CIVIL RELIGION
AND TRANSCENDENT
EXPERIENCE

CIVIL RELIGION AND TRANSCENDENT EXPERIENCE

Studies in Theology and History, Psychology and Mysticism

Edited by
Ralph C. Wood and John E. Collins
Wake Forest University

Religion and the Social Crisis III

Carlton T. Mitchell
Series Editor

The paper used in this publication meets
the minimum requirements of American National Standard
for Information Sciences—Permanence of Paper
for Printed Library Materials, ANSI Z39.48-1984.
∞

Library of Congress Cataloging-in-Publication Data
Civil religion and transcendent experience.
(Luce program on religion and the social crisis ; 3)
Includes index.
1. Civil religion—United States.   2. Psychology,
Religious.   3. Experience (Religion)   I. Wood,
Ralph C.   II. Collins, John E. (John Edward) III. Series.
BL2525.C58   1988   291.1'71'0973   88-5166
ISBN 0-86554-295-3   (alk. paper)

CONTENTS

PREFACE
Carlton T. Mitchell vii

CIVIL RELIGION IN AMERICA:
A RADICAL PROTESTANT PERSPECTIVE
John Howard Yoder 1

CIVIL RELIGION IN AMERICA:
A MAINLINE PROTESTANT PERSPECTIVE
Samuel S. Hill 25

CIVIL RELIGION IN AMERICA:
A ROMAN CATHOLIC PERSPECTIVE
David J. O'Brien 35

THE SEPARATION OF STATE AND CHURCH
AND THE RISE OF CIVIL RELIGION:
A JEWISH PERSPECTIVE
Manfred H. Vogel 65

THE CROWDED PUBLIC SQUARE:
A CRITIQUE OF RICHARD JOHN NEUHAUS
ON CIVIL RELIGION
Ralph C. Wood 85

TRANSCENDENT EXPERIENCE
AND PSYCHOLOGICAL MODELS OF THE BRAIN
John E. Collins 101

A NEUROPSYCHOLOGICAL COMMENTARY
ON BIBLICAL FAITH
Frank B. Wood 129

A QUAKER'S VIEW OF TRANSCENDENT EXPERIENCE
Douglas V. Steere 137

A CHRISTIAN WAY TO TRANSFORMATION
M. Basil Pennington, O.C.S.O. 155
CONTRIBUTORS 163
INDEX 165

PREFACE

This volume of essays is the third in the Luce Program on Religion and the Social Crisis conducted at Wake Forest University. A special grant from the Henry Luce Foundation enabled us to organize six symposia that sought to comprehend the complex relation between contemporary American religion and our present social calamity. The series was premised on the assumption that our society is in radical distress because, among other reasons, the various academic disciplines have fragmented into isolated specialties. The failure of scholars to enter into dialogue across the often narrow confines of their own expertise signals the loss, we believe, of any integrating center of social value and religious meaning. These essays are dedicated to the partial remedy of that failure.

They are also dedicated to the memory of Jon Reinhardt. Before an early death ended his brilliant academic career as a professor of politics, he was regarded as one of the keenest minds and most gifted teachers on the Wake Forest faculty. He won, in fact, the university's very first Excellence in Teaching Award. Together with Ralph Wood, he taught "Civil Religion in America," the initial seminar in the Luce series. This joint endeavor between the Departments of Religion and Politics provided lively student response for the public delivery of the first four essays here printed. The last three essays were also delivered as public lectures as part of a similar seminar offered by the Departments of Religion and Psychology. It was jointly taught by John Collins, a mysticism specialist, and by Frank Wood, a neuropsychologist.

Though civil religion and transcendent experience may not seem to share blood kinship, each topic serves in its own way to pose the profoundest of questions about the human condition, about the encounter with the Holy, and thus about the relation of religion to the contemporary social crisis. Professors Ralph Wood and John Collins, both members of the Wake Forest University Department of Religion, have added their own contributions to this discussion, thus rounding out a series of essays that we gladly offer to the wider world of scholarship and debate.

Carlton T. Mitchell
Series Editor

CIVIL RELIGION IN AMERICA:
A RADICAL
PROTESTANT PERSPECTIVE

John Howard Yoder

The planners of this series have placed before each contributor the embarrassing freedom to define what "civil religion" is supposed to be. If we were discussing the biography of some person, the meaning of some law, or the platform of some party, the objective definition of what we were talking about would be relatively similar for all of the perspectives from which we looked at it. "Civil religion," however, is no such thing. It is an analytical concept used by some people to describe something they like, by others to decry something they dislike, and by others to locate a phenomenon with value-free scientific objectivity. This variety within evaluative views does not prohibit their talking about the same thing, but it does put the definition under considerable strain. It has been pointed out that the people who were supportive of the fusion of religious language with civic values in the time of the civil-rights movement found themselves on the other side of the fence when Richard Nixon started having church in the White House. Martin Marty has identified two different scales of variation distinguishing what various major interpreters mean by the phrase; with typical creativity he entitled his analysis "Two Kinds of Civil Religion."[1]

---

[1]Martin E. Marty, "Two Kinds of Civil Religion," in Russell E. Richey and

One way to get past this built-in source of confusion would be to define a normative vocabulary. Yet that solution would be deceptive. The definition of the nature of the problem *should* probably be different from each perspective. I need, therefore, first of all to suggest in what sense it is important that we deal critically with one of the various phenomena that might appropriately be called civil religion.

The label assigned to me in this symposium—"radical Protestant"— also needs definition. I take it to denote the common thread of critical testimony addressed to "established religion" represented by the Czech Brethren in the fifteenth century, the Anabaptists in the sixteenth, Quakers and Baptists in the seventeenth, and their heirs in frontier America.[2] This view differs from some of the other postures represented in the series in two ways: first, because it is not represented by any hierarchy or scholastic elite, it can never be spoken for with full representitive authority; then, by virtue of its aggressiveness, especially in postfrontier situations, it may fall unawares into its contrary, into a form of informal establishment.

The marks of civil religion that matter for the purpose of locating the criticism with which I am concerned are the following:

First, the community that carries and is carried by a set of religious understandings and practices is a civil community: that is, one in which membership for most of its members is not voluntary, in which a function of coercively sanctioned organization claims jurisdiction over all the participants, normally within a territorial definition of physical frontiers and normally with a substantial degree of centralization of power.

Donald D. Jones, eds., *American Civil Religion* (New York: Harper & Row, 1974) 139-57.

[2]For our purposes it is especially important to recognize that the witness I have been asked to articulate is not that of a specific denomination but rather a perennial position taken, sometimes quite without coordination (in fact, often without any knowledge of one another), by scores of renewal communities—including a dozen major, independently viable ones—across the centuries and by renewal movements within established denominations as well. The concept of "ecclesiological type" is worked out by Franklin H. Littell in his *Free Church* (Boston: Starr King Press, 1957). The histories of some of the most representative examples are gathered by Donald Durnbaugh, *The Believer's Church* (New York: Macmillan, 1968). The use of the "type" concept for further analysis and illumination of history and contemporary churchmanship was begun by James Leo Garrett, ed., *The Concept of the Believer's Church* (Scottdale PA: Herald Press, 1969). The adjective "radical" assigned to this stance by historians refers not to specific social issues but to the degree of thoroughness with which one attempts to implement the reformation.

Second, the identity, welfare, and interests of this specific community, including the way those interests are recognized, defined, and implemented by the govermental powers, are thought of as appropriately a special concern not only of the citizens themselves but of the deity they invoke.

Third, the civil community is defined by its very nature to have outsiders and enemies. Such opponents are usually defined territorially, usually ethnically, sometimes religiously. Some of the major expressions of the alliance of God with the community's interests come at the cost of those "on the other side"—interests such as colonization, pushing back the frontiers, expelling aliens, and winning wars.

Fourth, other significant differentiae of moral or theological commitment, it is thought, should be set aside in order for the religious resources to have the desired supportive effect without being undercut by narrower "sectarian" definitions of loyalty and identity. Protestant, Catholic, Jew, and ethical humanist forget their differences and pull together. Confessional idiosyncrasies are demoted to the level of folklore. This common-denominator homogenizing effect led Will Herberg and others to suggest that we have here not a coalition of faiths but a new religion, significantly different from each of the particular traditions it claims to transcend and to fuse.

Fifth, it further follows backhandedly from the above, that, although no one ecclesiastical office or religious community can have distinctive standing or any claim to the support of the state, the clergy as a whole or the Protestant/Catholic/Jewish/humanist elite spokespeople as a class do carry a new version of the ancient status of "establishment." They have access, as a group taking turns, to subsidized chaplaincy services in public institutions. They reciprocate by assuring the powers-that-be of divine blessings in general and by reminding them occasionally of divine imperatives. The leadership figures of the religious and civil institutions generally recognize one another as peers and usually as friends, sharing in a complementary way the leadership of the wider society. This is represented in the symbolism of the Middle Ages by the legend according to which Pope Sylvester and Emperor Constantine exchanged documents and greetings ratifying one another's sovereignty. We might call such relations the affirmative side of the reciprocal recognition. The negative side was equally present in the medieval memory in the legend of Archbishop Ambrose of Milan, who held so much moral authority and political wisdom that he was able to discipline Emperor Theodosius for having committed a political massacre. In our age the positive form is probably best represented by the presence of religious figures pronouncing invocations at political events. (Until recently, almost no one seems to have noticed that many in the audience do not recognize such a member of the clergy as speaking for their faith.) The negative form may be seen in the authority seized sometimes by the clergy to speak judgmentally about major moral offenses within the political order.

By transforming the separation of church and state from the original notion of the Anabaptists, Friends, and Baptists, which had been rooted in the incommensurability of two orders, into the pragmatic fair-play notion of the Bill of Rights—namely, that no sect should have an unfair advantage and that the matter of establishment should be left to the several states—room was created for a new and more powerful version of the fusion of civil and religious covenants. The religious ratification of civil purposes thereby became all the more undisciplined, since the civil authorities could demand the allegiance of all the clergy in general but were accountable to none in particular. There is no longer a more-than-local manifestation of the people of God as a unity. No denomination or set of denominations with common views is such a unity. No patriarch or synod can talk back to the president or the Congress. Thereby the president becomes a modern Constantine, especially since we have no updated Sylvester to grant him his dignity and no updated Ambrose to upbraid him.

One could address a number of additional objections to this pious mainstream tradition from the perspective of radical Protestantism. I shall pursue those above that seem to be the most directly operational for present purposes, without meaning to exclude the others. Among those others, especially the following, not pursued here, would be worthy of more attention.

Sixth, radical Protestants have always been concerned for the inwardly authentic quality of personal experience and commitment. From this perspective one judges the run-of-the-mill piety that is satisfied with conformity to easily attained patterns of expression. This critical perspective on hypocrisy and superficiality presupposes a more authentic alternative, which is very difficult to define. Once it is clearly defined, that new, more authentic form becomes inauthentic in its turn; yet that kind of preoccupation always belongs as part of the radical Protestant vision. The civil religion is judged for being feasible; its demands are too attainable.

Finally, one would need to spell out, behind this potential for critique, the assumptions that the civil religion makes about the authority of Jesus Christ in relation to other authorities and the authority of Scripture in relation to other patterns of insight, or what is traditionally called the problem of revelation and reason. Here I intentionally have set aside that more systematic way of stating the problem, because of the amount of digression that would be needed to deal with it adequately. Nonetheless, it must be said that to proceed with the critical thrust described here, there must

be a knowable, definable Word—whether Jesus, the Bible, or the prophetic event—clearly set apart from common sense in its ordinary meanings. A civil religion, on the other hand, is commonsensical; it can have
no imperious Lord.

With more space, we could look more analytically at the interaction of
all the above seven traits, to ask whether one of them is more basic than
the others. Or are they all equally objectionable and for the same reasons?
Are some of the objections more important from the "civil" side and others from the "religious"? For the purposes of the present critique, I shall
posit instead the assumption that we are dealing, not with basically distin-
guishable traits that could be evaluated separately, but with multiple aspects of one global phenomenon.

THE "IDEAL" ALTERNATIVE APPROACH

I intentionally look at "religion" here as a multidimensional social
phenomenon rather than as one central religious idea. The obvious and most
traditionally attractive alternative would be to pay attention only to one such
idea or a set thereof. In the Declaration of Independence as a founding doc-
ument, it is said that all men are equal by creation and that this status gives
to them inalienable rights of life, liberty, and the pursuit of happiness. The
idea of a Creator is a religious idea, although it appears here in a somewhat
watered-down form. The idea that all people are bearers of rights is important for social criticism and construction. The very notion that a particular government should claim to be the incarnation of a philosophical
principle is radical in unprecedented ways. The use made of this founda-
tional affirmation by later saints such as Lincoln and King has given this
pair of phrases a special status. Is that idea itself our civil religion? My
choice not to use this kind of propositional focus for this analysis may need
explanation.

First, that statement did not, for the people who made it two centuries
ago, identify a genuinely transcendent fulcrum of judgment from which to
criticize their own culture. The "all men" in question did not include
women or blacks or original Americans. It reinforced, more than it criticized, the qualities of civil self-righteousness and defensiveness that I have
identified above as part of our problem. By attaching the appeal to the Creator to such a self-serving affirmation of rights, they also devalued the genuine transcendence that biblical religion insists on being judged by.

Then, the pop intellectualism that claims to derive institutions from a
few key ideas is wrong as a social science; such a use of religious ideas
cannot be right.

Third, although the language of "rights" can explain an insurrection,
it cannot create or govern a community. It cannot explain the realistic an-

thropology of federalism, checks and balances, and bills of rights, which had to move far beyond 1776 to create a viable government.

Finally, far more important than the genesis of an idea is the sociology of its carriers. Who are the people who will use such ideas as leverage for change rather than as a window dressing for privilege? Where will those people get their gumption and their social support? The question is one of community, not of the history of ideas.

More critically and creatively inclined people, including the two prominent prophetic Americans just named, in fact were able to use this phrasing as an instrument for a more fundamental criticism and reconstruction. Such ability, however, must be explained by reference to something other than what this phrase initially meant from the pen of Jefferson or in the politics of colonies breaking with the Crown; it is the wider and more critical reference that I am seeking to interpret. What made it possible for Lincoln and King to make a prophetic rather than a defensive use of the creed of 1776? It was not that creed alone.

ESTABLISHMENT AND ITS ANALOGUES

By setting aside this particularly intellectualistic interpretation of the "American religion," we have also prepared ourselves to move beyond the general description of our thesis to its historical location. Certainly a great originality of the great American system is disestablishment. The exercise of religion is constitutionally defended against infringement by governmental authority, and the establishment of religion is removed from the purview of the federal government. Does that safeguard not amount to a resolution of our problem, in contrast to the various patterns of church-state linkage and the subservience of the institutional church, which had dominated the European scene since the fourth century? We can better locate our present problem by observing how this apparent step forward was, on a more fundamental level, a step sideways: a deeper problem was avoided by means of a reformulation on the surface.

Here we have reached the root of the specific critique of national and public religiosity that accentuates its continuity with that ancient temptation, the submission to which radical Christians since the Middle Ages have been calling the "Constantinian fall of the church." In that profound, fourth-century redefinition of the meaning of Christianity, for which the first baptized emperor was to become a symbol, church membership henceforth no longer meant belonging to a voluntary community of disadvantaged, if not always actively persecuted, believers, but it became compulsory. The Christian hope beyond history was relocated, to be juxtaposed with the prosperity of the imperial throne. From this redefinition of hope and of community followed all the other redefinitions of hierarchy, cult, and morality, which later gave rise to the call for reformation.[3]

As the medieval synthesis ripened through the Crusades and the Renaissance, some called for reformation because the doctrines had gone wrong. Ideas were abroad that were counter to Scripture or to the Fathers. True enough, but why had the doctrines changed? Others called for reformation because the forms of church management and ritual had been deformed. These critics rejected the papacy or pompous and formal worship or the medieval understanding of the Eucharist. True enough, but why had they gone wrong?

Still others called for change because the Church's moral vision had been lost; bishops tolerated or even implicated themselves in the avarice of simony and the violence of the Crusades. True again; but why had they arisen? The answer of the Waldensians in the twelfth century, of the Czech Brethren in the fifteenth, of the Anabaptists in the sixteenth, and of the Baptists and Friends in the seventeenth was that "establishment" was the error behind it all. I wish here to explicate the perspective that views the fault with American civil religion not only in its manner of being civil but, even more primordially, its manner of being religious.

Concerning each of the already-identified traits of the phenomenon, I thus need to demonstrate, in ways that others of any persuasion should be able to understand, that American civil religion is civilly bad, and in ways that make sense biblically, that is is religiously bad. Before proceeding with that exposition, however, I must ward off one persistent misinterpretation, which claims that the only way for a religious critic to be consistent is to admit irrelevance to the political realm.

---

[3]See my interpretation of "Constantinianism" as a sociocultural reality independent of the fourth-century details, in *The Original Revolution* (Scottdale PA: Herald Press, 1971) 150 ff., and in "The Constantinian Sources of Western Social Ethics," *The Priestly Kingdom* (Notre Dame IN: University of Notre Dame Press, 1984) 135-47. To understand the symbolic meaning attached for centuries by radical Protestantism to the name of Constantine, attention must be directed not to the man but to his veneration by later "established" historians and churchmen as one who initiated the age of the church's prosperity. This made him the symbol of the epoch of the great revival; dissenters have simply judged the change negatively instead of positively. The point was not that he was a man of blood, not that they doubted the spiritual authenticity of his conversion or the propriety of his convening the church councils and dictating the wording of their creeds but that he inaugurated the age when Christianity became the official religion. Cf. Leonard Verduin, *Anatomy of a Hybrid* (Grand Rapids: Eerdmans, 1976).

CRITIQUE IS NOT RETREAT

Those who consider themselves to be moderate or responsible in the custodianship of any majority tradition commonly grant room for criticism only by the patronizing maneuver of relegating it to the fringes. The "saint" and the "prophet" will find ready recognition from such moderates, but at the price of the concession that their critical vocation is heroic, and not to be taken as normative for others, nor as a judgment upon the unavoidable responsibilities that others must take upon themselves. Not only is the individual "vocational withdrawal" into irrelevancy granted a backhanded recognition; the moderates will recognize as well collective withdrawal by monasteries and Mennonites, friends of nature and Rechabites, whose collective rejection of some element of some dominant culture is recognized as having moral merit, with the proviso that it is worthy of respect only in correlation to the degree of consistency with which the withdrawal is carried through. These midstream persons who are willing to grant the moral integrity of vocational withdrawal, however, do not recognize the possibility that they might be challenged on moral grounds not from the fringes but from within the system that their centrism is claiming to administer. It is therefore of fundamental importance that the radical Protestant view I discuss here is neither individual vocational purism nor communitarian countercultural withdrawal but a challenge to the established system upon its own turf.

The error represented by the establishment, as primordially a theological offense, comes first, in the order of logic, to say that it is wrong for the church to be established. It is, however, no less wrong for a wholesome civil order that it should establish a religion. Therefore the denunciation of establishment occurs as much for the sake of the health of the civil community as in the defense of the fidelity of the religious community. Such denunciation is a service to society, not a retreat into purity.

The most pernicious effect of the Constantinian concubinage is not that it permits provincialism and community self-centeredness to go on. They could go on anyway. The worst is not even that God is made responsible for the mixture, though that is blasphemy. God is used to that. The worst damage is done by the system when it dictates the terms in which the critics can respond to it, casting their criticism as a mirror image of what they reject, rather than seeing that they refuse the standard formulation of the issue. This happens whenever free churchmen let themselves be told they must be anticultural or apolitical. The alternative to Christian nationalism is not religious treason but more constructive—because more critical—reconception of the values a national community should stand for. The alternative to idolatrous patriotism is not *un*patriotic. The alternative to the fusion of Christ and culture is not a Christ rejecting culture but a more radically Christ-oriented transformation of the genuine values hidden amid the mishmash called culture. The alternative to the neo-Constantinian fusion of church and national power is not withdrawal to the ghetto, the desert, or the *bruderhof* but the discovery of the next frontier, where a more honest dialogue between the community of faith and her neighbors can build a more open pattern of civility. The alternative to buying into the power game as it is being played is not opting out but inventing a new game. I would therefore have been falling into a trap if I had sought to formulate a simple negation by saying (assuming that we had solved the earlier problem of a common definition) that, whereas some others consider civil religion good and others call it ambivalent, I know it is simply wrong. Such a simple negation would be tributary to the wrong way of putting things that it sought to reject. I must condemn not the seeing of nation and power as important or as a theme of religious concern and theological interpretation, but the particular ways in which that concern is shaped and in which that interpretation proceeds.

The issue is thus not one that can be clarified by a mere ruling as to how we should use words. Sidney Mead has preferred to use the phrase "the theology of the republic," which means for him a perspective more critical than the religious patriotism of others.[4] Any improvement, however, is because of Mead's own wise civility, not because the words are better. The question is one not of phrases or of agenda but of direction. Is Christian participation in the costs and responsibilities of citizenship, insofar as those are accessible, a matter of claiming God's support for our purposes, especially the defensive and self-centered ones, or of pleading our support for God's causes? Neither a reassuring slogan like "responsibility" nor an alien one like "distance" can help as such. We need to look at cases.

The alternative of inventing a new game instead of buying into the power game according to its old rules is not a pipe dream; it has been at work in the past. Over against the blind-alley models of Puritan establishment in New England and Anglican establishment on the southern seaboard, the free churchmen Roger Williams and William Penn (no less practical for being guided more by their churchmen's experience of the faith community than by England's experience of royal authority) were first not

---

[4]Daniel F. Rice, "Sidney Mead and the Problem of 'Civil Religion,' " in *Journal of Church and State* 22 (1980): 53-84; and Richard T. Hughes, "Civil Religion, the Theology of the Republic, and the Free Church Tradition," ibid., 74-87.

only to envisage but also to create a commonwealth with religious freedom, where the original Americans were recognized in the dignity of their
languages and tribal culture. As Franklin Littell said in his insightful dash
through American religious experience, *From State Church to Pluralism,*[5]
when Christianity in America sees itself as the youngest of the Christian
nations of Europe, it renews the racist-nationalist sins of the old country
with the vigor of youth. When, on the other hand, we see growing here the
oldest of the younger churches, then the leverage offered in North America
for cultural creativity is unparalleled.

The line goes on through the underbrush at America's growing edges.
There were William Lloyd Garrison and Alexander Campbell, holding together abolitionism and nonviolence. There were William Jennings Bryan
and Norman Thomas and Harold Stassen, perennial near-winners, seeing
their victors soon defeated and some of their causes winning. There was
Judge James E. Horton, who in 1933 sacrificed a judicial career in the attempt to give a fair trial to a black man. There was Martin Luther King,
Jr., utterly Baptist when, almost despite himself, he became the most important churchly instrument of cultural change in our century. Most of them
Baptist, most of them pacifist, most of them who would rather be right than
president: they were the heralds of creative cultural change on a national
scale precisely because they did not conceive the national power as their
goal but kept their eyes on the higher loyalty of kingdom citizenship.

A stereotypical notion—that a Christian commitment governed by such
more critical and more promising visions drawn from the experience and
the witness of the Christian community can properly be categorized as
"apolitical" or "unrealistic" (as was done in the heritage of Ernst Troeltsch
by the brothers Niebuhr)—thus misreads the facts. A more demanding and
more promising vision is not unrealistic just because it calls for risky faith.
It would be unrealistic if it sought to impose desired behavior on others in
the absence of conviction to support it (as in the national detour with the
prohibition of beverage alcohol). It would also be wrong if faith in due
process and in the wholesomeness of tolerating dissent was identified with
Christian commitment. But those are established mistakes. Neither did
they—and here is the discrimination misunderstood by the Niebuhrian
analysis—conclude that, because faith cannot be imposed, they should retreat to a world (or even to a church) where there would be only believers
or that, because humane decency is less than the gospel, it should be written off.

---

[5]Franklin Littell, *From State Church to Pluralism* (Garden City NY: Doubleday
Anchor, 1962).

IS RELIGION NECESSARILY A GOOD THING?

One strand of critical perspective that demands attention is the increasingly open doubt that has been growing in different directions for the last century about whether the best way to talk about Christian faith is to put it within the wider category of "religion" at all. The strongest thrusts in this direction, after having been strongly stated earlier in our century, have been displaced by some more recent fads and trends, but not because they were soberly refuted.

There are profound reasons for doubting the clarity and therefore the adequacy of the term "religion." Without assuming that all possible meanings merit our acceptance, I owe it to the dialogue to allude here to the half-dozen ways in which it has been seriously advocated that Christianity is best not understood as "religion" or as "one of the religions."

There is a significant difference, although we need not pursue it at length here, between the two phrases just used. To suggest that Christianity is "one of the religions" is to posit a larger class, all of the elements of which are somehow similar in their basic structure or function, with their common features being more fundamental than their differences.

On the other hand, one may talk about the Christian faith as "a religion," without paying attention to all the others. Then one gives to that term a meaning that is assumed to be understandable in itself as a part of Western culture, since the time when in the fourth and fifth centuries Christianity replaced the kinds of religion that had been operative in the Roman world. In this view we do not compare Christianity with any living analogues but rather describe its place in Western culture, from which the other ("false") religions have long been preempted. This approach says that Caesar cult or sun worship has been displaced but not that Buddhism and animism are of the same genus.

Since the others are held to be "false" and ours is "true," established Christianity may be (as far as Western thought in the Middle Ages is concerned) the only one of its kind. Therefore when we say Christianity is a religion we need not ask about the others. Hendrick Kraemer, in his *Christian Message in a Non-Christian World,*[6] worked out most carefully the implications of the line of questioning already being directed against this view by Europe's "theology of crisis" in the 1920s and by the "theology of the Word" in the 1930s. If God is really God and not a projection of our best intentions, if we are really sinners and our ability to know any-

---

[6]Hendrick Kraemer, *The Christian Message in a Non-Christian World* (New York: International Missionary Council, 1947).

thing (or at least divine truth) is negatively conditioned by the warping of our own wills against the truth of God, and if the message of the gospel is that God has acted in ways we could not fully predict, could not do ourselves, and cannot even adequately reflect upon in our own wisdom, then any response to this kind of message from God must on rigorously logical grounds be radically distinguished from the kinds of human behavior that in all societies express the efforts people make to come to terms with the complexity of life, to manipulate unseen powers, to find God by much searching, or in any other way to replace the simple acceptance of pardon by pure grace with some kind of human performance.

From this perspective to become a "religion" is the abiding temptation of Christianity rather than its essence. This critique of Kraemer's sees its polemic precursors in the argument of Augustine against Pelagius, or of Martin Luther against medieval Catholic works-religion, or of the "theology of crisis" against liberal humanism. Christians may do religious things, but in so doing they are no different from pagans. Specific to biblical realism, says Kraemer, is the absolute subordination of the things Christians do and the ideas they cultivate to the prior action of a God whom they could never reach on their own and whom, in fact, they have no criteria for accrediting. Human efforts to reach the divine, including ascetic disciplines intended to get us out of the way and to facilitate the Divine's reaching us, are all the kind of self-salvation efforts that Christian faith condemns as pride. Not only do they work at the wrong task; such efforts exaggerate and escalate the basic problem, namely, the epistemological presumption of our claim that we shall know truth when we see it if only we work a little harder at finding it.

Christians indeed also do the kinds of things that "religions" lead people to do: they pray, theorize about the transcendent, and meet psychic needs—but such efforts do not make Christian faith Christian. Those activities, when seen in themselves or in what they do for a person, are rather the temptation to faith than its nature.

This pattern of criticism by Kraemer and Karl Barth was a part of the breakthrough of recognition in the 1930s that old patterns of interpretation of Christianity as a "typical" human phenomenon was not adequate. By no means, however, was this critique the first of its kind. It seems rather that this critique made it possible that earlier ones, which had not been honestly faced or which had been observed but feared and ignored, could also now be given attention. This recognition now meant reaching back all the way to Feuerbach, who was one of the first to draw the most thorough conclusions from the observation that a religion is a human activity, making God in our image or in the image of what we decide we need.

Barth also opened the door for some moderately respectful attention to Marx's critique that religion has the defensive social function of weakening the critical perception that the poor might otherwise have developed of the injustices of their own existence and thereby defending the class interests of the people in power. It is no surprise that Barth was a socialist. He agreed with social conservatives that Christianity had in the past been used to defend existing power relationships.

Barth noted even the cultural critique of a man like Nietzsche, for whom religion, as a network of references to the transcendent, cuts the nerve of a human dignity that ought to be affirmed in its own right. Barth did not have to reach back even that far to make some room for Freud's critique that religion is a special kind of illusion or compensation phenomenon that has the psychodynamic function of making sense of a world that becomes increasingly confusing as we grow up in it. Whether we focus on Freud's own further definition of the needs it meets as predominantly sexual or go other directions with Adler or Jung or Erikson, in any case religion is explained "from below" as an immature, human performance.

Dietrich Bonhoeffer in prison, probably in conscious development of ideas initially encountered in Barth, elaborated his own critique of religion as the backdrop of a worldview. On the personal level, Bonhoeffer criticized what he called methodism. This term meant not the denomination but the view of many that, to win individuals for the Christian faith, one must speak to them at the point of their weakness. One who makes this assumption is then predisposed to attend to the shadow side of human existence, the dimension that proves that "something more is needed." Such methodism jumps on people when they are down; it proves the need for God by proving that we are no good without God. For Bonhoeffer, this approach is the opposite of the gospel itself, which tells people, especially outsiders, about the love and goodness of God for its own sake and does not try to convince people of their misery or their guiltiness. Only if it is *not* seen as a response to weakness, is the gospel really the good news of the love of God as Creator, Sustainer, and Savior. Apologetic approaches that try to make the point of human weakness and ignorance and lostness are hopeless, not because they do not say something true, but because what they are interested in proving is not the good news.

The last phase of the reception and updating of the critique of religions was found in the early writings of Harvey Cox and in parallels and echoes about the same time as the publication of his *Secular City*.[7] For the early

---

[7]Harvey Cox, *The Secular City* (New York: Macmillan, 1965); and Daniel Callahan, ed., *The Secular City Debate* (New York: Macmillan, 1966).

Cox, "religion" represents a normal, stable worldview focusing upon the otherworldliness of basic reality. This preoccupation with the other world undercuts the importance of historic Christian reality as fact and as mission, since it continues to claim that the higher reality is somewhere else than in history.

Behind all of these recent critiques of "religion," appealed to as a precedent by some of them, is the original Hebrew rejection of the religions of Old Testament days—the great cosmic/imperial cults of Babylon and Assur and the local fertility deities of Canaan's hills. The first Christians reaffirmed that Jewish heritage and proclaimed it across the Mediterranean world, denying respect to the Hellenistic pantheon and obeisance to the divine Caesar. The theological name for misdirected religion is *idolatry,* "worshiping the creature instead of the Creator." The civil community, with its values and its power structure, is as good a specimen as we can get of such a creature that should properly be respected, used, and even honored—but not sacrificed to.

Yet another dimension of the religious, one that the cultural anthropologist would make more of, is the unique status it gives to a few special persons: the shaman, the priest, the seer. Set apart by heredity, by initiation, by education, or by peculiar disciplines, that person renders to the society a service of linkage to the divine world that all the others gladly pay for. Over against the vocationally separated definition of the religious person, there stands the laicizing impact that Hebrew faith had upon the ancient Near Eastern religions, early Christianity upon Hellenistic and Roman religions, and radical Protestantism upon the sacerdotalism of medieval and magisterial Christianity. Even a secularized and pluralistic culture still has a special slot for "the clergy."

The last form of this critique of religion centers on the agenda of the community. Priestly religion attends to the limits of manageable life: mortality and mystery, facing death and catastrophe. Or it celebrates rhythm; its ritual follows the yearly cycle of the crops or the life cycle that goes from birth to puberty, marriage, parenting, and death. Prophetic faith cares about ethics and politics—righteousness in history, poverty, power, and justice—which it refuses to leave to the politicians by making the religious another plane.

What do all of these criticisms of so-called religion lead us to? First of all, I emphasize that I am reporting here the witness of Christian theologians, who "do theology" because of their concern with the authenticity of Christian faith. I am talking not about freethinkers, skeptics, Enlightenment critics, or professional doubters, but about accountable professional theologians who, for reasons of integrity and evangelism, are concerned to distinguish the Christian message itself from some of its broad equivalents and from its most evident counterfeits.

It is not true that any religion is better than none—that, for example, all "religionists" should close ranks over against "secularism" or "irreligion." Nor is it true that religion is all right, just as long as it does not get too involved in politics. Rather, most religion is idolatrous, and some of it is blasphemous. The first duty of churchmanship and of theology is thus vigilance against wrong religion. As a part of that vigilance, one must denounce insufficiently critical attention to the intrinsic presumptuousness of civil powers and provincial communities.

The several critics of wrong religiousness whom I have cited were not centering their attention expressly on the civil realm. They were working at other facets of the theological task. Yet as each of their critiques applies with special aptness to the civil temptation and becomes most understandable, meaningful, verifiable, applicable to the real situation, then it is specifically at the line between civil religion and authentic belief that the particular kind of critique they call for would begin.[8]

THE ALTERNATIVE

The first thing wrong with civil religion, on my list, was making the faith community involuntary. On this point, the American system preceded the rest of the world in pulling out of the medieval synthesis. It was possible for our governments to decontrol the churches, thanks to Roger Williams and William Penn, whose first concern was for the authenticity of free-church allegiance. They determined as churchmen to decontrol the state. The first British Baptists and Friends did not want religious freedom as a better form of government; they wanted free, adult membership as the right way to be church. In that insight they went beyond the New England theocrats, who used the same language about the church but remained Zwinglian, or Calvinistic, about government. It can hardly be our theme here to review, as if it were news, the case against infant baptism (although it is news today in Reformed Switzerland, in Lutheran Germany, and in Roman Catholic liturgical renewal circles). This is, however, the time to renew the warning that the fusion of evangelical language with political

---

[8]Not that this dividing line is the only such frontier. The religiosity of individual self-fulfillment without constitutive critical social awareness (represented by Dale Carnegie's churchly counterparts, especially as they become allied with sanctification of "the market" or "enterprise" as producers of prosperity) is a major temptation. The neooriental and neoarchaic cults will constitute perennial fringe phenomena, more attractive as the sense-making functions of mainstream religiosity fail to convince. But most of these other more bizarre "religious" sideshows do not—as the civil religion does—move people to kill one another.

neoconservatism—which right now claims to be gaining ground elector-
ally with the avowed design of again putting the power of the civil sword
behind the preservation of white Anglo-Saxon Protestant values—threatens to be one more tragic rendition of that ancient mistake, all the more
tragic when the media ministers leading the campaign are nominally Baptist. We cannot ask of civil society that its membership be voluntary. But
we must continue to object when the institutional separation that all modern democracies have now achieved is belied by a continuing psychological equivalent of establishment.

The second mark of the civil religion, on my list, was the invocation of
the God of the Bible to bless this community in a way that redefines the very
character of the God we understand him to be. The definition of transcendence determines the difference between the religion of the nation (into which
established churches fall) and Christianly accountable kinds of theological
grappling with the meaning of the nation, which classically has been done by
free churches. If the God-reference of civil religion is inward or upward, it
provides no effective leverage for critique or transformation. The God-language of the Bible does not point inward to the renewed heart alone or upward
to the "higher power" or forward to the "hereafter" but backward to the salvation story, outward to the claims of the rest of the world (including the enemies to love and the slaves to be free), and forward to a city not of our own
making. Of these directions, the historical reference stands to teach us the most.
Only this direction will stand still to be counted. The irreducible historicity of
Abraham and Moses, Jeremiah and Jesus; the demonstrable wrongness of
Constantine and Charlemagne and the Crusades; the providential rightness of
the renewals, spoken for by Peter Waldo and Peter of Chelcic, Fox and Bun-
yan, Penn and Williams, of the call to obedience to a God whose sovereignty
is not at the service of human dominion but who, rather, calls human power
into servanthood—these are the memories that can best give substance to our
hopes. The transcendence that counts is not a power from beyond that is now
leashed to favor us but the affirmation of values beyond our control to which
we are committed, calling us to be ministers of peace and of justice above,
beyond, and maybe even against our own interest. Ask not what God can do
for America; ask what America owes humankind. This observation applies as
well to the most valid of the less churchly theologies, like that of Lincoln.

The references thus far to God as transcendent, beyond our situation
in time or in space, can become concretely effective within the civil community only if represented by a discrete empirical community, what we
call the free church. All of the language of transcendence is but rhetoric
unless there is a visible body of people who are able to escape conformity
to the world while continuing to function in the midst of it. Their confes-

sional commitment to living according to the transcendence we have been considering enables, and in turn is enabled by, their social visibility. The insistence upon the baptism of adult believers, which led some people to be called by their persecutors "anabaptist" in the sixteenth century or "baptists" in the seventeenth, was not the fruit of a psychologically preoccupied concern for the age at which it is possible for a person to have a valid religious experience. It was the sociological prerequisite for forming in the midst of the world a community of nonconformists whose culture and character cultivate an alternative construction of the community's history. That community is different from the surrounding community not because, like so many groups of immigrants in the American melting pot, they came from a different part of the Old Country but because of the allegiance they confess to Jesus as Lord, over against other lords.

That God's transcendence is moral and not only metaphysical, that the differentness he demands is justice and not otherworldliness, is part of the reason no institution can claim his rubber stamp. The church can speak for God only under the proviso of forgiveness and subject to the contradiction of others. No government can speak for him, no nation can count on his aid in its selfish pursuits or identify its adversaries as his enemies. Thereby we are driven on to our third point: the God of the gospel loves his enemies.

The beginning difference between the nationally defined vision of human dignity and the biblical one is the place of the outsider. The Abrahamic covenant begins with the promise that all the peoples of the earth are to be blessed. The early centuries of Hebrew experience seemed far from that goal, with the exclusion of the Egyptians and the Canaanites in particular and of "the enemy" in general from the scope of saving concern. Yet the story moves steadily toward the inclusion of all nations. The concern of the Mosaic laws for "the stranger in thy gates," Jeremiah's acceptance of the dispersion, Paul's mission to the Gentiles, and Jochanan ben Zakkai's acceptance of the fall of the second temple are only the most notable of the milestones along the way to the deterritorialization of the believing community. "They take part in everything as citizens, and put up with everything as foreigners. Every foreign land is their home, and every home is a foreign land."

It seems clear that, in the *ordinary* meaning of "civil religion," the American experience has always needed the polar outsider to precipitate a common self-awareness: the savage, the slave, the infidel, the "hun," the "Jap," the godless Communist. Our own ethnically mixed society perhaps demanded the foil of a racially polar bad-guy nation to reflect upon ourselves a borrowed sense of natural unity.

The challenge is simple: if we accept the traditional territorial definition of the community under God, we deny the unity of the human race in creation, the cosmopolitan reality of the church in mission, and the eschatological vision of the world in redemption. The alternative is to accept the claim that this nation—any nation, every nation—under God is called to multicultural reconciliation internally and to practical humanitarianism globally. Is it too much to ask of the United States that national interest be seriously qualified by commitments to the dignity of other nations and peoples, acknowledged in the form of real claims held by others upon our cultural and economic resources? If we are willing (as I fear we are) to leave it to the Swedes and the Canadians to project internationalism as a realistic policy, then let us at least not burden the God of Abraham with our provincialism.

I mention territorial provincialism first, in order that it be clear that the offense against the world vision of the God of Abraham and Jesus is first of all more than a matter of dollars and lives. The first question is who the humanity is whom God loves. The most dramatic expression of our provincialism is obviously not our general xenophobia or our disregard for other languages and cultures. It is not even our neocolonialism. It is that, with a good conscience and with the resonance of congressional bipartisanship, we continue (even in an age of national belt-tightening) to escalate our investment in the capacity to destroy, by the hundreds of thousands if need be, the citizens of nations we have let someone declare our "enemies." At the same time that we make those peoples the hostages of our nuclear targeting or of our discriminating acceptance of "moderately repressive" dictatorships, we state our convictions that the governments that rule over those people do not speak for them and are not morally legitimate.

If the military expression of our nationalism is the most blatant, perhaps in peacetime its commercial expressions are more concretely destructive. The multinational corporation is in fact not even subject to the controls of one particular government. In a broad cultural way, however, it is the fitting expression of the patterns of morally uncommitted rational exploitation to which the "free enterprise system" commits its advocates, with the maximizing of profits finding a transnational terrain freed even from the antitrust regulations that capitalistic nations enforce domestically. My concern here cannot be to analyze the good or the evil that these entities commit but only to recognize that, as a portion of our society sees in them a celebration of the special worth of our peculiar American economic system, we have raised provincialism to a global scale in the economic realm, as we had already done in the realm of military technology.

It will not ward off this concern to say that, in judging military patriotism, I speak from the bias of a perspective that even since Constantine has been resoundingly voted down by majority Christianity. I am not now making a pacifist point. The war now being prepared for is condemned by the so-called just-war tradition held by most Christian theologians since Ambrose. Obliteration bombing has been condemned by every pope since Benedict XV, by every major gathering of the World Council of Churches since 1937. It does not first become a sin when lives are taken. It begins to constitute idolatry when the particular interests of a given national regime are deemed worthy of our contemplating and threatening the destruction of another people for the sake of such interests. The idolatry crescendos when our best brains, dollars, minerals, and energy resources are invested in tooling up for it, when the media and the schools are enlisted to rationalize it. If we considered such destruction in the name of *avowed* self-interest or the virtue of the Aryan race or the market economy, at least it would not be a blasphemy against the name of the God of Abraham.

As the free-church witness calls for decision from the individual, so it sets before the community not one way but two. With regard to territorialism as such, and again with regard to military nationalism, I have said we must look both ways. We might on the one hand assume that our context is pagan. Our rulers could admit, as political scientists of the style of Hans Morgenthau and Ernest Lefever do, that the basic interests of a nation should be selfish. That position would have the virtue of honesty. But then it would become clear that the nation cannot call itself Christian, or Protestant/Catholic/Jewish/humanist. The believing community should then set about, as it does today in Asia and Eastern Europe, living the life of faith in a culture it does not control. The other way, which would be a challenge and a choice (not a chaplaincy), would be to call the civil community to renounce short-range self-interest as a goal and global arm-twisting as a means of defending what we claim are the values of Western civilization.[9]

After the collapse of the slightly sanctimonious international optimism of the early Carter era, it may need to be underlined that a radical Christian judgment on American nationalism is not the same as naïveté. One of the differences is the relation to national pride. There was a parallel between President Carter's earlier claim to "make the government as good as the people" and his dramatic insistence throughout the Iranian crisis that the United States had no apologies to submit to anybody. It is not from a posture of self-proclaimed innocence that the second-biggest bully on the globe

---

[9]The values that can be defended by means of global arm-twisting are those not of Western civilization but of the good guys who always talk our language, shoot straighter, and turn out in the end to have been on the right side when they had to break some rules along the way. The Western, together with its near neighbors in police and spy drama, educationally celebrates the cultural values in which our society trusts. In such a world the fastest gun determines who is moral.

can teach moral lessons to smaller countries with more oppressive regimes but also more poverty.

The fourth mask of civil religion is its homogenizing disregard for the particularities of different traditions. The peculiar things some Jews do about food and about Saturday, the Lutherans' understanding about grace and the Baptists' about baptism, the special ideas some Evangelicals have about Jesus and some Catholics about his mother are all relegated to the status of dispensable folkloric appendages that we should not mind losing from view behind the pieties of the melting pot.

I note this mark with less emphasis, because others can concentrate their defenses there and because I cannot say that there are not some particularities that are worth submerging in a larger ecumenical stream. On the other side of the relationship, however, it must be noted that the ceremonial content of the civil pieties is most thin and sectarian and petty: the Memorial Day rereadings of the Gettysburg address that lose their note of repentance and tragedy, the various references of politicians to prayer, the nondenominational blessings invoked on flags and battleships, the trust in God that our money announces but our investment policies do not. The pieties of the melting pot do not, despite the hopes of Robert Bellah, give a community enough to live from.[10] The civil cult is a narrower, not a wider, church.

The fifth mark of bad religion I named was the status of clergy as privileged: not as servants of particular, voluntarily constituted and accountable communities, but as a clerical caste within the society as a whole. Instead of "free exercise of religion" meaning the space for individuals to pray and for groups to be constituted, it has been transmuted into the right of clergymen in particular to diverse discounts and tax advantages, or to the right of the bearer of a clerical collar to be treated differently by the police watching a protest march.

Radical Protestantism is not anticlerical in the sense of rejecting theological learning or doctrinal precision, but it does insist that the status of a "minister" is defined by an accountable relationship to the community he or she serves, and not set apart because of the "religious" quality of the language or rites involved in that ministry. Nor does radical Protestantism oppose the involvement of "the ministry" in public life, but it asks that

---

[10]See "The Birth of New American Myths," in Robert Bellah, *The Broken Covenant* (New York: Seabury, 1975) 139ff. Although Bellah projects such a hope, his overall concern, like Mead's and like mine, is to be critical of the same things I condemn. Bellah does not use the term "civil religion" in his more recent writings.

what they say be honest and representative. Ever since Jeremiah's judgment on those who promised a too superficial peace (Jer. 6:14; 8:11; 23:16-22), like before him Micaiah ben Imlah's condemnation of the prophets of well-being (1 Kings 22; 2 Chron. 18), the most authentic contribution the spokespersons of God can make to the wider society will most often not be the soothing reassurance in the face of mortality and crisis that a society expects of its priestly servants. The more authentic troubling word is not one that the wider society will readily listen to, or pay for. Witness the rapidity with which Christian agencies are threatened with the loss of their tax-deductible status if their expressions of politically relevant moral preferences are too blunt.

The issue focused here, however—namely, the abiding respectability of clergy even in a secularized society—is only the tip of the anomaly. Despite the secularization of learning and despite the secularization in *substance* of the criteria of public decision-making about such matters as the dignity of human life, there remains a veneer of God-language over public discourse in the United States. Oaths in the name of the God of the Bible (which in its text tells us not to swear such oaths) are still part of the rituals of induction into high office. The less that political figures let morality interfere with their decision-making, the more freely they will claim transcendent reference for their view of the nation's interests.

Once again the radical Protestant critique will not seek a Rechabite return to the desert but will demand that, if God-language is used, it be specified and that, if there is appeal to the God of Abraham and Jesus, there be submission to his revealed will regarding the liberation of the oppressed, the dignity of the outsider, and the unity of the race. Especially the correlation of God-language with provincial, national, or class self-interest will be consciously rejected and reversed.

I do not mean to say that negative prophecy is the only authentic public message. There may be times more desperate than our own, in which only believers can hope and Christian dissent will consist in sharing that hope. In the current American experience, however, the challenge is at the point of national self-confidence, gluttony, and pride.

My assignment here has thus far not seemed to call for direct dialogue with others who use the notions "civil religion" or "theology of the republic" affirmatively or who support the same position without using the words. The challenge they need to face is how that particular distillate of the national experience can be an instrument of genuine moral judgment as well as of consolation and encouragement. If one commends such a religion or theology as somehow "true," one must face all the hurdles any missionary faith must meet. Why should it be believed? How does it work to judge and to restore? Does the sociological fact that a coherent cohesive society *needs* a coherent value system, argued by Robert Bellah at the end of his *Broken Covenant,* prove that such a system can actually be created or will be believed? Does Sidney Mead's own critical civility in wanting a "theology of the republic" to be self-critical[11] guarantee that the nation can affirm the crusading self-righteousness of the "Battle Hymn of the Republic" and still retain the tragic humility of Lincoln?

To take the advocates of civil religiosity more seriously would mean clarifying who their founders and church fathers are and what their canon is, beyond a few phrases from 1776. My efforts to understand these colleagues are frustrated because they do not sense the need to explain on what grounds, beyond taste and civility, they prefer the perspective of Lincoln and King on the national identity to that of the Ku Klux Klan and our gunboat diplomats.

To take more seriously the theological exaltation of the republic would also demand accountable reference to the ecumenical challenge. What is the relation of this vision of salvation and national calling to the rights and dignities of the rest of the world? To other religions? To other Christians? There may very well be good answers to these questions. In the debate of the last decade, it is significant that the advocates of the nationalist answer have betrayed no awareness of the need to spell out answers to such challenges before their claim to credibility can be granted.

Our subject is therefore, by the nature of the case, as ambivalent as when we began. If by "civil religion" should be meant the bare fact of our caring Christianly about public life, then the message would be the same as it is to an individual: a call to repentance, to the recognition of God's sovereignty, and to a commitment to live for the service of others. We should then have a positive Christian call to address to all public life. The radical Protestant version of that call would differ not in being unconcerned or impossible but in being more ready to run risks for the sake of a higher justice. But when what is usually meant is the religious undergirding of national interests at the expense of the wider righteousness, then the technical word for that offense, even if the name of Jesus be invoked over it, is *idolatry.* "Why do you call me 'Lord' and do not do what I say?"

We call a nonviolent man Lord and in his name rekindle the arms race. We call a poor man Lord and, with his name on our lips, deepen the ditch

---

[11]See references in note 4.

between rich and poor. We call Lord a man who told us to love our enemies, and we polarize the globe in the name of Christian values, approving of "moderate repression," as long as it is done by our friends. The challenge of civil religion is not a fact to which we chould choose whether to say yes or no; it is an agenda. Is God, above all, our help? Or are we God's servants?

CIVIL RELIGION IN AMERICA: A MAINLINE PROTESTANT PERSPECTIVE

Samuel S. Hill

What is the relation between mainline Protestantism and the American civil religion? Has America's historically dominant faith contributed to, or been involved in, or simply tagged along with, the so-called civil religion? On any assumption that the civil religion exists, we may be sure that mainline Protestantism is coimplicated with it.

At the same time we may be quite certain that the nation's central religious tradition has been among the most suspicious forces in the society concerning the civil religion. Its statistical and cultural strength has assured the former; its basic perspective, its very heartbeat, has fostered the latter, except when it has denied its own character. Moreover, on the issue of the civil religion, mainline Protestantism includes not only the denominations belonging to the National Council of the Churches (white and black) but also nearly all black Christianity, the Southern Baptist Convention, and much of the constituency of the white sects.

Perhaps it will be useful to list five recognized meanings of the term "civil religion" and indicate the meaning when I use it. Civil religion is *folk religion,* something that emerges out of the life of the folk and becomes an idolatrous faith in competition with traditional religion. Civil religion is *religious nationalism.* This is the religion of patriotism, in which the nation is the object of adoration and glorification. Civil religion is *the democratic faith*. On this view, equality, freedom, and justice are exalted, yet without necessary dependence on a transcendent deity or a spiritualized nation. Civil religion is *Protestant civic piety*. This meaning amounts to the fusion of Protestantism and nationalism. Finally, civil religion is *the transcendent universal religion of the nation*. In this last usage, which is the standard one in this paper, civil religion functions as a source of meaning and social solidarity for the nation. It is a way of understanding the American experience.[1]

To sharpen the definition for focus here, I am treating the civil religion in America as drawing upon American experience yet not ideological, as having a transcendent quality without being ultimate, as existing alongside the received biblical faiths but not in competition with them. It is a dimension of American culture that features symbols and values for our common public life (a phenomenon, in fact, whose existence cannot finally be "proved" by either historians or sociologists).

Let us be clear that "civil religion" is a specific interpretation or instance of an issue that confronts all societies, namely the relation between religion and politics. Both deal in ultimates: politics claims the power to make life-and-death decisions, while religion claims to derive from an authority that transcends all earthly powers. The crucial questions in any particular case have to do with how politics and religion are correlated. Are they the same because they are undifferentiated? Are they differentiated yet the same? Are they separate and parallel? Are they separate and remote? In this vein it has recently been argued that the American case is unique inasmuch as here political legitimacy and political ethics exist but are not fused with either church or state.[2]

Those who have planned the Luce Series have acted wisely in conceiving of it in comparative terms. Most discussions of the topic have been less sensitive on this score. It matters greatly what the black community, historically powerless, thinks about the reality and the healthfulness of this feature of our society. Likewise, we should heed the voice of Roman Catholics, whose own attempts at Americanization netted them limited success until perhaps the 1930s. For my own part, I regard the response of Jews and radical Protestants as the most significant and telling. Modern Jewry has

---

[1]Russell E. Richey and Donald G. Jones, eds., *American Civil Religion* (New York: Harper & Row, 1974) 14-18.

[2]Robert N. Bellah and Phillip E. Hammond, *Varieties of Civil Religion* (San Francisco: Harper & Row, 1980) viii-xi.

generally believed the world's response to Judaism to be a kind of barometer of the health of society worldwide. In America, where the public schools occupy such a formidable position, Jews are the sector of the population best attuned to how free this society is, how respectful we are toward dissenters. And let us remember that dissenters in this case means people who are not simply strange, or a nuisance, or objectionable, as with Catholicism between the 1830s and World War II, but who are truly deviant, espousing a hopelessly aberrant religion in addition to comprising a cluster of alien ethnic peoples.

The radical Protestant perspective is particularly important because it brooks no compromise, thereby embodying in specific the general vision of mainline Protestantism. We may expect the most searching critique of political idolatry, or anything that flirts with heresy, from the Mennonites, the Amish, the Hutterites, and their kin—that is, when they get around to voicing their convictions on the topic. Better known for their life-style than for theological utterances, for attending to their own affairs than for assuming responsibilty for the whole, radical Protestants prefer to practice a live-and-let-live philosophy. But their clear commitment to spiritual authority over political authority may issue in prophetic pronouncements when there is a hint of rivalry between the two authorities. Moreover, the practice of an alternative life-style, best exemplified by the plain-and-fancy Amish and the world-renouncing Hutterites, may be more than simply freezing seventeenth-century European customs as some charge them with. On the contrary, it may be contended that the burden of proof falls on those who adapt. In other words, radical Protestants in America, because they may have the clearest understanding of the relation between spiritual and worldly authority, may be the wariest of all about civil religion.

The salience of the roles of various minority cultures in the United States takes nothing away from mainline Protestantism's position, however. Even a brief listing of its contributions to the conditions that helped produce the civil religion is impressive. First, the original Puritan vision was that the new commonwealth was holy because it was the New Israel. Such a perception of things is heady, magnificent in its boldness and promise, potentially frightening in its implications. Our destiny is special, unique; is it also superior? *Special destiny* is one ingredient in the civil religion construct. Second, from the beginning there were varieties of Protestants. By the 1780s, there were all the kinds in the United States that there were anywhere in Europe, plus Catholics and Jews. Yet to come were those that our culture was to generate. Mainline Protestantism thus supported and encouraged *diversity* as an ingredient in the civil religion complex. Third, *decentralization and social atomization* were ingredients in the emergence of a civil religion. Even if the multiplicity of sects had not taken root here, Protestantism would likely have forsaken centralization and establishmentarianism.

This third contribution of mainline Protestantism to American civil religion—its preference for localism and individualism—calls for more attention, since that proclivity has not always been manifest. At least certain parts of colonial New England had been a Europe-like state-church society. While that pattern of church-state alliance was never universal and did not last long, it lived on, modified, in the Calvinist concern to bring the whole created order, most especially its social institutions, under the dominion of God's will. The notion of Christian responsibility to infuse, transform, and give direction to the public life of the society did not die out. It persists to this day in mainline Protestantism and, unpredictably in many cases, even among some fundamentalists and many Evangelicals.

But if a notion of civic responsibility did not die out, it certainly receded from a position of dominance. By the middle third of the nineteenth century, organized church religion was tending to "go private." Protestant Christianity was talking about and acting on its convictions that true religion is "personal," meaning individualistic, having to do with religious experience and personal morality, with the church seen as the aggregate of the regenerate. As a great deal of recent research has shown, however, personal religion was intended to make good citizens, a healthy public order, and a Christian nation. The strategy had changed, from direct efforts by colonial Calvinists to make church and state partners in the building of a holy commonwealth to the later interpretation that "good people make a good nation." But the vision of America as the New Israel, as a people with special destiny and unique calling, remained. Moreover, a wistful attitude surfaced toward the good old days of a stable Protestant society without Catholics, issuing in some efforts to keep our society pure and in others to Christianize the westwardly expanding population. Thus, in altered and sometimes subtle ways, the dual Puritan focus on the regenerate individual and a righteous society held fast.

Paradoxically, Protestantism's public program helped generate the civil religion. Phillip Hammond observes that the development of a civil religion in any society depends on circumstances "allowing persons and institutions to be 'religious' and 'political' at the same time. The heavenly sphere of theology must blend with the worldly sphere of the civil."[3] Drawing upon Max Weber's analysis, Hammond argues that the universal tension between politics and religion tends to be diminished under certain conditions, by innerworldly asceticism, for example. Among Calvinistic Protestants especially, the old form of self-denial that was institutionalized

[3]Ibid., 78.

in the controlled life of the monastery gave way to the rigorous, intro-
spective conscience of Christians who were living within ordinary society
and believed themselves to be much responsible for it. When innerworldly
asceticism shapes the Christian vision, political structures can be "instru-
ments for the . . . ethical transformation of the world and for the control
of sin." In consecutive aphorisms, Hammond highlights Protestantism's
contribution to creating a context for the civil religion: (1) "Where medieval Catholicism politicized religion, American Puritanism sacralized
politics"; (2) "The Puritan way of resolving tension between religion and
politics left the church, *qua* church, with no power, therefore, but it meant
religious symbols entered politics."[4] Such a threshold is easy for a civil
religion to cross. As in no other society, such an entity did develop under
these American conditions.

More needs to be said, however, about where and why civil religions
develop. They are superfluous in societies that have (or once had) a mon-
archy or a state church. Where those institutions or their residues exist, in
societies where state and government coincide, the power of societal symbols and of cultural cohesion provides the features contibuted by a civil
religion in other kinds of societies. There, offices and officeholders, traditional authority, and ceremonial occasions and trappings keep things familiar, on course, and in place. In the United States, not even the most
powerful or charismatic president or famous or effective religious leader
can fulfill those functions. In one sense, things are never really "familiar,
on course, and in place."

Robert Bellah is surely correct in identifying surrogate occasions and
functionaries in this society: for example, Inauguration Day and the Fourth
of July; Washington, Jefferson, and Lincoln; the Constitution; and the flag.[5]
Such surrogates do not possess the status held by monarchies and religious
establishments, to be sure, but they are real, and their force is significant.
We turn to Hammond again for clear understanding of what happens in a
society, like the American, where a civil religion may develop.

(1) The condition of religious pluralism prevents any one religion from being used by all
people as a source of generalized meaning, but (2) people nevertheless need to invest their
activity with meaning, especially when that activity brings together persons of diverse
religious background. Therefore (3) a substitute meaning system is sought and, if found,
the people whose activities have been facilitated by it will tend to exalt it.[6]

4Ibid., 79-80.

5Robert Bellah, "Civil Religion in America," in Richey and Jones, *American
Civil Religion*, 28-29, 32-33.

6Bellah and Hammond, *Varieties*, 121-122.

Hammond further clarifies how that exalting takes place and what its real impact is. In some societies legal order exists in its own right but gets a helping hand from informal sources. The agencies of the legal order in those societies use the "language and imagery of purpose and destiny." They "not only resolve differences but also *justify* their resolutions." When conditions like these prevail, something identifiable as a civil religion can very easily emerge.[7] Stated differently, when, to an already existing "clergy," "rituals," places for "worship," and a number of directions for behavior, one adds a "theology," that is, an "ideology of purpose and destiny or theodicy," one has a civil religion in the making. American society may be the quintessential context for such a development.

"Purpose," "destiny," "theodicy," and "justification" are concepts reminiscent of the biblical outlook of the settling Puritans, the evangelizing frontier missionaries, the peace-seeking President Wilson, and the containment-minded supporters of the wars in the 1950s and 1960s. We can only conclude that mainline Protestantism played a part in the injection of these highly symbolic concepts into the bloodstream of American life.

In summary, mainline Protestantism, by the very nature of its historic role in the creation of American society and through forms its symbolic life takes, has made a sizable, perhaps decisive, contribution to the elusive reality called the American civil religion. It has done so partly by helping to create the sort of context in which a civil religion can grow and partly by providing symbolic concepts such as "destiny," "purpose," "New Israel," and "special Providence" to describe the national experience.

This conclusion, however, is predicated on something easy to overlook because it is disarmingly obvious. I refer simply to the basic acknowledgment that the civil religion exists. Before the civil religion is promise or peril, it is a fact, an identifiable dimension of our common life, even if, instead of Robert Bellah, we prefer John Wilson and his denial that it is a "developed and institutionalized religion," "a separate and differentiated religion," "a religion identifiable alongside other possible cults in society," "a reification."[8] A civil religion does exist in American society, but who besides mainline Protestantism would have been likely to note its lineaments? I suspect that the historic religious underclasses or out-groups, such as Catholics, Jews, black Christians, or sectarian fundamentalists would not. Nor is it likely that students of American political institutions,

---

[7]Ibid., 136.

[8]John F. Wilson, *Public Religion in American Culture* (Philadelphia: Temple University Press, 1979) 144-45.

history, and symbols would have detected its presence. The fact that Americas's dominant faith has been up to its ears in civil religion, as source, promoter, and sustainer, would seem also to have equipped it to discover this feature of our society.

We have noted mainline Protestantism's role as contributor and, quite briefly, as the community that, by acknowledging civil religion, has brought the concept into public view—an achievement that makes possible our reflection on it as fact, promise, or peril. But mainline Protestantism has played also the role of critic. Having helped create the civil religion and having held it up for notice, mainline Protestantism also assesses it. I illustrate this point by recalling Congressman Walter Fauntroy's reply when aked why he attended the congressional breakfast sponsored by the National Religious Broadcasters. He replied that he was present as "prophet and judge." As a black minister, and therefore as a member of the mainline Protestant community, he attended this largely New Right occasion in order to address consciences and represent an alternative Christian viewpoint. Mainline Protestant leaders who have led the charge against equating America with the kingdom of God have been armed with a copious supply of pins for pricking the balloon of American self-inflation. One thinks of John Bennett's description of Protestantism as a precarious way; of Reinhold Niebuhr's fear in the early Nixon years that Billy Graham, the putative prophet, could be seduced by the atmosphere of the king's court; of Richard Niebuhr's brilliant treatment of the dialectic between order and movement, with Protestantism favoring movement; of Paul Tillich's "Protestant principle," that nothing in history is absolute, nothing earthly is worthy of final devotion.[9] Both the Presbyterian Bellah and the Unitarian Mead have insisted that a civil religion (or "religion of the republic," as Mead prefers) is not inherently—and must not become—idolatrous.[10]

With these direct criticisms of chauvinism, or American nationality, or societal idolatry, is bound up the particular way American society correlates process and program—that is, liberal constitutionalism and classical republicanism.[11] I confess that my own sentiments and convictions run to

---

[9]In particular, see H. Richard Niebuhr, "The Protestant Movement and Democracy in the United States," in James Ward Smith and A. Leland Jamison, eds., *The Shaping of American Religion* (Princeton: Princeton University Press, 1961) 22-24.

[10]Sidney E. Mead, "The 'Nation with the Soul of a Church,' " *Church History* 36 (September 1967): 262-83.

[11]Bellah and Hammond, *Varieties,* 8-10.

republicanism, by which virtue is promoted and citizens produced. Yet it is not difficult, even under modern pluralistic conditions, for the virtues and the nature of the ideal citizenry to be determined by some for all, as the example of the New Religious/Political Right makes clear. Such movements do not come to terms with the basic issue of what is morally acceptable in a pluralistic world. Accordingly, we do well to have the liberal spirit as part of our equation, to protect and provide for the rights and freedoms of individuals, even if they are primarily economic rather than political and moral. The civil religion tilts toward republicanism, as seen in its rootage in presuppositions of transcendence. It is committed to program, that is, to substance and goals, but also to process. Trading as it does principally in our symbol and value life, it succeeds in escaping the trap of engineering a single program by which all Americans are expected to live their lives. Process as well as program characterizes American democracy and the civil religion in their ideal manifestations—and, in measure, mainline Protestantism also.

We turn to still other, sometimes paradoxical and ambiguous, areas of relation between mainline Protestantism and civil religion. Mainline Protestantism has helped to set the context for and to create the civil religion. It has stood on the Archimedean site from which it has been able to view, acknowledge, and describe this phenomenon of our culture. It has engaged in criticism of any and all idolatries, including the United States of America as an idol, a position into which the civil religion can shade off, indeed a position taken by some whose outlook is one version of the civil religion. My impression is that most Protestant-minded interpreters in this country either doubt that a civil religion exists or equate the phenomenon so named with religious nationalism or folk religion. That is to say, some regard the idolizing of America as the primary issue raised by the civil religion, and others simply do not see, or perhaps fail to take the pains for developing the vision to see, the "transcendent universal religion of the nation." Personally, I could wish for better, since I do believe that civil religion points to something real that, not being inherently perverse, needs acknowledgment and improvement.

Two other connections in the complex linkage between Protestantism and the civil religion deserve mention. First, some mainline Protestants are guilty of complicity in the view that America is superior. These we may call the complacent party. Then, the politically minded within the Protestant right wing believe that America is God's chosen nation. These are the fundamentalists. The first group, the complacent, do belong to mainline Protestant churches and, in many cases, are meaningfully at home in that religious community. But the classic Protestant message of scrutinizing all human achievements and loyalties in light of the one transcendent loyalty has not struck their lives with force, at least not with regard to the nation. Their tendency is thus to go along with a civil religion or a folk religion of a religious nationalism sort, its tone being quiescent, compliant, uncritical, ease-taking, sometimes imperious.

It is a different case with the second story—the Protestant right wing, or fundamentalism—but the net result is the same. Here there has long been a tendency to see America as a special, if not superior, nation. But "Special" in this setting means status as well as calling—America is special and is called to a special mission. And thus the nation has a double grip on the position that may result in uncritical loyalty to America understood as ideal. This issues in a curious consequence. On the one hand, the hard-hitting preachments of right-wing Protestantism make it the most likely, in theory, to be critical of any nation-over-God notion. At the same time, however, this group is highly susceptible to being victimized, in practice, by an America-is-God's-nation ideology. Despite disclaimers about not "wrapping the cross in the flag," there is a marked tendency to act on the conviction that, if the world is to be saved, America must do it, or that the moral and spiritual stakes are higher in America than anywhere else.

I note also a growing national habit that strikes me as potentially dangerous: namely, the personification of America, the use of the noun "America" in direct address. Common examples run quite a range: "Good morning, America"; "Thumbs up, America"; "Come to McDonald's for breakfast, America." As far as I know, no other national society so conceives of itself. Perhaps this usage is innocuous and related most notably to the massive size of our advertising industry. Or it may have its roots in this diverse people's continuing need to forge a social unity. But occasionally I fear that we may believe ourselves metaphysically to have a kind of solid, permanent existence. This notion is not a political concept as the civil religion is, but since it is social or perhaps cultural in character, it too operates in the public domain and may be pernicious.

Finally, my assessment of the American civil religion is made not so much in terms of its promise or peril as in terms of its reality in our common social existence. This approach is correlated with my understanding of it as the transcendent universal religion of the nation. It seems to me that we are confronting a social reality created by centuries of American experience that no amount of wishing or of concern can eradicate. American society is destined to feature two kinds of religion, one of church and synagogue, the other of public symbols. I concur in John Wilson's insistence that our civil religion is not highly developed, institutionalized, or differentiated. But it or something like it is there, out there and in here, as a "common symbol horizon'' (in Wilson's phrase). One of mainline Protestantism's chief roles is to help keep the civil religion within proper banks, preventing it from spilling over into the lowlands of folk religion or religious nationalism.

Surely, the civil religion bears improvement. I propose that it would be considerably improved if Americans developed a more sensitive awareness of American history and American government. This growth would include a more critical, less adulating, reflection on our nation and its life. It would also mean the transmission of more stories, more narratives, more lore, without which a Western-style religion cannot flourish. It would mean greater attention to comparative and international studies. Furthermore, it suggests increased involvement in the ceremonial life of our political society. It may even mean that educational curricula should include more means by which symbols can be studied, perhaps through anthropology and sociology. Also, since I regard republicanism as having greater depth than liberalism, I hope we will rededicate ourselves to the teaching and inculcation of moral values, in the interest of producing citizens. After all, if we are destined to have a functioning civil religion, we may as well make it the best it can be.

CIVIL RELIGION IN AMERICA:
A ROMAN CATHOLIC PERSPECTIVE

David J. O'Brien

The historian who once compared writing intellectual history to nailing jelly to the wall had not yet experienced the slippery qualities of civil religion. A sociologist describes a Long Island volunteer fireman whose peak experience came when he rode in the white Cadillac convertible at the head of the Fourth of July parade, and calls that incident civil religion. Another scholar connects the note of ultimacy in drug culture with the frontier images of American literature and labels the bundle civil religion. On Inauguration Day, 1981, while American hostages were returning from Iran, the Mormon Tabernacle Choir serenaded the new president with "The Battle Hymn of the Republic," a black choir sang "Free at Last" outside the modest Detroit home of a freed American, and in the basement of a Colorado church, a Chicano family offered a Mass of Thanksgiving for the release of another. Here we have a kaleidoscope of American images united with logic-less spontaneity—a collage of the nation and its infinite variety of peoples as Ronald Reagan promised deliverance from economic decline and national weakness and Americans rejoiced at the return of their fellow citizens; the emotions on the faces are civic and seem religious.

That America might be a "nation with the soul of a church" is, in Norman Mailer's words, "either the best or the worst idea ever to shake the mansions of eschatology in the world beyond," but it is an idea that touches something deep in the national consciousness.[1] At once exciting and frustrating, this constant interaction of personal and collective experience with intuitions of transcendence opens up horizons that, once approached, immediately recede. Images of America fuse memory and hope, moving minds and hearts; when examined, however, those images become the historian's jelly. Scholars labor to define the nature of the experience, the meaning of those moments when private anxieties fade a bit and Americans peer out on the vistas of long-cherished dreams and see things differently. Mailer, America's most gigantic ego, at the end of the ritual march on the Pentagon in 1967, saw in twenty naked Quakers in a Washington jail cell the nation's hope for redemption. Five years later, the insight was clearer: "In America, the country is the religion. All the religions of the land are fed from that first religion, which was the country itself."[2]

In America, the country is the religion. Can the Christian imagination respond with anything but revulsion? Can the Roman Catholic church, that everlasting symbol of universality, ever say yes to America in quite that way? The church may perhaps be an unwitting participant, like John Cardinal Krol in Miami in 1972, offering an oration of praise to the Christian nation and standing arm in arm with Richard Nixon and Spiro T. Agnew, singing "God Bless America." Or it may supply a prophetic critic, like the Jesuit Daniel Berrigan, tasting to the full the sweet wine of America and having it "turn bitter as gall" in his mouth, the very bitterness reflecting the sweetness of a nation loved too much. Must not the church, any church, stand further apart than the self-appointed national priest and prophet? Is not the Catholic always an outsider at the banquet, asking when, if ever, this "almost chosen people" will join the human race and face the ambiguous realities of poverty and wealth, virtue and sin, life and death?

Must not Roman Catholics always be, as John Courtney Murray insisted, heirs to symbols and possessors of truths wider and deeper, wiser and more true, than the parochial symbols and deceptive half-truths of America? One part of the contemporary Catholic intelligence answers "Of course!" "We are not allowed to have a divided allegiance," John Garvey writes. "Our allegiance to America is allowed only as long as it is consis-

---

[1] "The nation with the soul of a church" is a phrase first used by G. K. Chesterton and is examined by Sidney Mead in *The Nation with the Soul of a Church* (New York, 1975) 48-77. The Mailer quotation is from *St. George and the Godfather* (New York, 1972) 87-88.

[2] Mailer reflects on the Quaker prisoners in *The Armies of the Night* (New York, 1968) 318-19.

tent with the following of Christ.''[3] No respectable Roman Catholic would disagree, and none today unequivocally affirms the civil faith. Yet, there was 20 January 1981, and some of those Americans who felt very good about themselves and their country were Catholics. The American question, then, for Catholics as for others, is not a question for the mind alone; it lies somewhere beneath and beyond both theology and politics, in that realm of feelings about past and present, meaning and purpose, celebration and sacrifice—in that dimension of human experience we have learned to name religion.

CATHOLICISM AND THE CIVIL RELIGION

The relationship between Catholicism and the civil religion remains a vast, unexplored territory. To begin to map out the landscape, we will confine our attention to church leaders, especially bishops, and to that aspect of civil religion commonly called nationalism. By this term I refer to the claim of the nation, frequently made through the state, on the ultimate allegiance of all its citizens. In the United States, such nationalism is frequently articulated in terms of the unique, special character of *this* nation and its providential destiny to bring about liberty and progress on earth. In order to fulfill its unique responsibilities, the United States has to ensure unity among its diverse peoples and enlist them in the service of its special mission. In this chapter we will confine ourselves to the response of Catholic leaders to this nationalism, ignoring for the most part the popular reflection on personal and communal experience in light of transcendent realities, which accompanied the evolution of collective American symbols.

In the early stages of its history in the United States, the church's leaders attempted to define a middle ground, shaping a Catholic subculture that would be neither too Catholic (that is, too European or too papal) nor too American (that is, too indistinguishable from other faiths or from the national culture to inspire loyalty, dedication, and sacrifice). In the wake of the Civil War, however, a new breed of leaders, called Americanists, challenged this cautious, balanced approach. They began to speak of the nation in providential terms, and they developed a program designed to bring the church to full participation in national life. To do so, they developed an understanding of the Catholic role in America that drew heavily on the national symbols of liberty, progress, and destiny. Their ideal contradicted the teachings of the universal church, and their policies threatened the careful balancing of traditional Catholicism and American ambitions re-

---

[3]John Garvey, "Does God Always Bless America?" *U.S. Catholic* (April 1981).

quired by a Catholic population that included native Anglo-Americans, converts, and assimilated Irish Catholics but that was constantly increasing through the migration of Catholics from Europe. The Americanists were eventually defeated, and their ideas were condemned, as a newly reorganized church adopted strategies of organized alienation comparable to those of the European church but lacking the latter's disdain for democracy or its desire to restore a premodern integration of Catholicism and public life.

Instead, American Catholics claimed to have the resources to "re-Americanize America," a position that helped provide a distinctive Catholic identity in the United States without requiring any particular brand of politics. Catholic nationalism in the twentieth century was a public piety, not a democratic faith; in no way did American experience criticize or test the church, nor was the possibility of conflict between civic loyalty and religious integrity even admitted. With Vatican II, however, a democratic faith reemerged as some Catholics once again attempted to bring their church more energetically to the service of their nation's ideals and mission. In the period that followed the council, that hope was all but destroyed by the conflict between the (1) need to preserve a distinctive Catholic identity grounded in separate institutions and, (2) a radical disillusionment with the country, expressed in a sectarian withdrawal from serious engagement with the national culture.

Today, the absence of confidence in the nation and faith in its people is reflected in the weakness of church leadership, the aimless contentiousness of intrachurch disputes, and the absence of vigor and energy in the middle-class Catholicism of suburban churches and Catholic colleges and universities. If the American churches are, in Mailer's words, "staggering across deserts of faith," it may be because they have, like him, found the nation they loved too much to have been "false, ill and corrupt." If so, then the Catholic church may require a reconsideration of its American role and responsibilities if it is to recover a sense of purpose and play a creative role in the universal church and in the nation.

THE EUROPEAN CATHOLIC RESPONSE TO MODERNITY

In nineteenth-century Europe, Roman Catholicism found itself in the unaccustomed role of an outsider in nations that had once been Catholic. Faced with challenges to its authority and in danger of being driven from the center to the margins of life, Catholicism clung tenaciously to the privileges of the ancien régime. The prospect of minority status was simply unacceptable. To meet the challenges of secularization, the church attempted to solidify its position by unifying its scattered forces, strengthening clerical discipline, gaining control of episcopal appointments, breaking the power of independent national hierarchies, and, ultimately, reducing local churches to outposts of an ecclesiastical empire centered in an infallible papacy and a strong central administration in Rome. Where a majority of the people were Catholic, the church attempted to define a legal relationship with the state that would ensure its independence and its influence over education, culture, marriage, and family life. In countries with non-Catholic majorities or anticlerical governments, the church used its new solidarity and discipline to create a coherent Catholic subculture, with its own churches, schools, charitable organizations, and social, cultural, and apostolic associations and movements. In both cases, the church used its influence to resist the inroads of secularism, materialism, and liberalism among its own people and, as far as possible, in the nation as a whole.

Church leaders deliberately rejected the proposals of men such as the French reformer Félicité de Lammenais that they jettison the cultural baggage of the past and join the struggle for human dignity that the Reformers believed was at the heart of the democratic revolution. Instead, they chose to preach "obedience to subjects and justice to rulers," to demand recognition and status for the church, to present her as the champion of tradition, order, and authority, and to tighten ecclesiastical discipline, clarify the boundaries of orthodoxy, and construct a rigid, self-contained Catholic culture.

Although it was on the defensive in the nineteenth century, the church embarked on a campaign for reconquest in the twentieth. Leo XIII deepened the philosophical and theological foundations of ultramontane Catholicism and urged political flexibility and ministry to the workers in order to reclaim lost ground, all the while demanding the most rigid control of lay action. Leo XIII and his successors invited unstable states and frightened people to consider the benefits of Catholic restoration. He was not alone in believing that "the tranquility of order and true prosperity flourish among those people the church controls and influences."[4]

Parliamentary democracy seldom allowed such control, and multi-party systems seldom allowed such influence. The church, secure in its possession of truth, had little patience with such conflict-ridden systems. "Amid the strife of political parties," Pius XI wrote, "the very foundations of authority have been swept away by removing the primary reason by which some have the right to rule, others the duty of obedience." Hav-

---

[4]Leo XIII, "On Christian Democracy," in Etienne Gilson, ed., *The Church Speaks to the Modern World* (New York, 1957) 328.

ing driven the church from power, there was no longer "any supporting, safeguarding stay, nothing left but factions fighting for command among themselves."[5]

Nationalism, the church's enemy in the nineteenth century, became its ally after World War I. In Italy and Austria, in Spain and Germany, nationalism offered a route to Catholic restoration, while Catholic opposition to liberalism sanctioned resistance to constitutional government. Conservative ideology and ecclesiastical self-interest might on occasion require criticism of statist extremes, but always the church championed authentic national rejuvenation. Patriotism was a recognized Christian virtue with clear duties: commitment to national unity, extension of Catholic influence, and collaboration with legitimate governments, that is, governments that gave protection and offered recognition to the church.[6]

The Catholic church ambiguously resisted totalitarian efforts to erect patriotism into civil religion, liberal in France, Bolshevik in Russia, fascist in Germany; but it championed the fatherland, taught obedience, and yearned for restoration of a Catholicism recognized in civil law and integrated into civil ceremony.[7] Pluralism and toleration were considered naive and destructive; in the long run, unity of religion and culture, church and state, was indispensable to the health of church and nation. Stable governments and secure societies required religion—one religion—and that religion was as prepared in the twentieth century as in the eighteenth to offer its services to the state. "Since, then, the profession of religion is necessary to the state," Leo XIII wrote, "that religion must be professed which alone is true."[8] Alternative civil religion, legitimate and fully acceptable, could be fulfilled only by cooperation with the one, true church of Christ.

Modern Catholicism therefore saw the modern world, its people, and its institutions as prizes in an age-old battle between the church and anti-Christian forces. While tactics and strategies changed, Catholicism before Pope John XXIII resolutely refused to consider a more positive under-

---

[5]Pius XI, "On the Peace of Christ in the Reign of Christ," in Terence P. McLaughlin, ed., *The Church and the Reconstruction of the Modern World* (New York, 1957) 34.

[6]See John J. Wright, *National Patriotism in Papal Teaching* (Westminster MD, 1956).

[7]For example, see Guenter Lewy, *The Catholic Church in Nazi Germany* (New York, 1964).

[8]Leo XIII, "On Human Liberty," in Gilson, *Church Speaks,* 71.

standing of the secular order. Joseph Comblin summarizes the historical experience forcefully.

In the preconciliar days . . . the Popes accepted secularization as an unfortunate but indubitable fact. It was the result of errors which Satan had inspired in heretical Christianity and modern philosophy. The work of the Church, consequently, was to wage war against these forces of destruction in the hope of restoring the medieval order. In the nineteenth century . . . the Church's struggle had been viewed as a heroic defensive action. The Church would stand firm against assault, winning by the weight of her inertia. . . . With the rise of Catholic Action in the early days of the twentieth century, the Church was already thinking in terms of reconquest. Her task would be to restore the social order of Christ the King. Even Maritain's notion of replacing sacral Christianity with a profane Christianity did not radically alter this perspective. The Church's task was to "consecrate the world to Christ," rendering it obedient to his sovereignty.

The only thing that would change would be the means to this end. No longer would the Church seek to re-establish a Holy Empire of neo-Catholic nations. Now it would see that reconquest could be achieved through democracy. Yet, all during this period, the world was seen as inert matter, waiting to be shaped and ordered by Christian forces. History was still seen as a process of decline and restoration, with Christianity the only active, positive force.[9]

CHURCH, SOCIETY,
AND GOVERNMENT IN THE UNITED STATES

In the United States, things were different, but not altogether different. Here the church was on the outside from the start and had no hope of restoration, but it found such a position beneficial and regarded the world around it with confident optimism. The first generation of Catholic leaders were practical and enlightened men who walked a tightrope between a Catholicism that seemed too foreign and authoritarian and might excite anti-Catholic animosity and an Americanization that might jeopardize the unity, discipline, and doctrinal coherence of the church. The Maryland Catholics who organized the American church made great sacrifices to preserve their faith, but they kept their religion private and unobtrusive. In life-style and culture they differed little from other planters of the Chesapeake Bay region. Cosmopolitan, tolerant, Federalist in politics, they supported the Revolution, had doubts about the War of 1812, and suspected the Jeffersonians of Jacobin tendencies.

John Carroll, appointed the first bishop in 1787, spent half his life in Europe and there witnessed the destruction of his beloved Jesuit order. Carroll regarded the new arrangement of religious affairs in the United

---

[9]Joseph Comblin, "Secularization: Myth and Real Issues," in Roger Aubert, ed., *Sacralization and Secularization, Concilium,* vol. 47 (New York, 1969) 125.

States as more significant than the political revolution. He urged his followers to conduct themselves "with the utmost prudence" so as to give rise to no suspicion of their dependence on a foreign power or lack of loyalty to the Constitution. Carroll and his successors skillfully maneuvered to keep Roman officials at arm's length, they downplayed the role of the papal office, and they eventually won firm control over the appointment of new bishops for the American mission. At the same time they mixed easily with Protestants, often sharing facilities for worship; they experimented with English liturgies and generally won respect for their enlightened views and civic dedication.[10]

Nevertheless, the early bishops were by no means enthusiastic Americanists. They well knew that they must establish episcopal authority or risk absorption into democratic, Protestant America. They ensured unity and orthodoxy by establishing firm control over the appointment of parish priests. Battling lay trustees who challenged that right, Carroll warned that lay control would mean that "the unity and Catholicity of our Church would be at an end, and it would be formed into distinct and independent societies, nearly in the same manner as the congregational Presbyterians of our neighboring New England states."[11]

For well over half a century the bishops fought the trustees, willing to accommodate lay participation but consistently opposing lay control. Lay militants used republican symbols to support their cause before the non-Catholic public, but the bishops were equally insistent that their spiritual authority in no way contradicted American values of liberty and equality. When John England tried to nationalize his diocesan experiment in constitutional government, which gave the laity a strong advisory role, the rest of the hierarchy was opposed, but few bishops agreed with Ambrose Marichal that England's program was wrong because it was "democratic," with "shepherd made subject to the flock."[12] Rather, they concluded from practical experience that only their clear-cut control of clerical appointments, and therefore of church property, would enable the church to survive; Catholic distinctiveness alone could inspire the voluntary support

---

[10]On Carroll, see Peter Guilday, *The Life and Times of John Carroll* (New York, 1922); Joseph P. Chinnici, "America Catholics and Religious Pluralism, 1775-1820," *Journal of Ecumenical Studies* 19 (Fall 1979): 727-46.

[11]John Carroll to Thomas Stoughton and Dominic Lynch, 24 January 1786, in Thomas O'Brien Hanley, *The John Carroll Papers* (Notre Dame, 1976) 1:204.

[12]Quoted in Peter Guilday, *The Life of John England* (Westminster MD, 1954) 357.

needed in a pluralistic society where neither the state nor wealthy patrons could provide money or protection. The early bishops, by creating an episcopally dominated church polity, set their stamp on, and set limits to, the American character of Catholicism in the United States.[13]

The church, then, was to be Catholic, but not too Catholic; American, but not too American. In ecclesiastical affairs the bishops and clergy established unique prerogatives, but in social and economic life they welcomed and promoted their people's active participation in secular affairs. "The priests in America have divided the intellectual world into two parts," de Tocqueville noted. "In the one they place the truths of revealed religion, which command their assent; in the other they leave open truths which they believe to have been left open." As a result, he told his European readers, "There are no Romish priests who show less taste for the minute individual observances, for extraordinary and peculiar means of salvation, or who cling more to the spirit and less to the letter of the law than the Roman Catholic priests of the United States."[14]

Even more striking was the bishops' acceptance, and indeed celebration, of political liberty. They lost no opportunity to emphasize their own independence and that of their people. In 1829, John England told the Congress of the United States that he knew of "no tribunal in our church which can interfere in our proceedings as citizens" nor of "any portion of the American family more jealous of foreign influence and ready to resist it." Government claimed no dominion over "spiritual or ecclesiastical concerns," England said; the church, for its part, "would not allow to the Pope, or to any bishops of our Church, outside our Union, the smallest interference with the humblest vote at the most insignificant ballot box."[15]

Yet, the problems of Catholicism and America were not so easily resolved. Many Americans honestly believed that Catholicism endangered the Republican experiment and threatened the goal of making America "a holy nation and a godly people." The acceleration of Catholic reaction in Europe lent support to their fears. Archbishop John McCloskey noted that the Syllabus of Errors, published in 1863, "places us in a state of apparent antagonism, as far as our principles are concerned, to the institutions under which we live, and affords a grand pretext to the fanatics who are anxious

---

[13]Joanne Manfra, "The Catholic Episcopacy in America, 1789-1852" (Ph.D. diss., University of Iowa, 1975).

[14]Alexis de Tocqueville, *Democracy in America*, ed. Richard D. Heffner (New York, 1957) 154.

[15]On England's Speech to Congress see Guilday, *England*, chap. 34.

to get up a war against us.'' He noted wistfully that it was consoling to think that the Pope was guided by the Holy Spirit, "for, according to all the rules of mere human prudence and wisdom, the encyclical with its annex of condemned propositions could be considered ill-timed."[16]

Then and later, the bishops and theologians could reconcile this "apparent antagonism" only by denying the possibility in the United States of a civil religion. As Martin Spalding put it: the First Amendment "simply lay down the sound and equitable principle that the civil government, adhering strictly to its own appropriate sphere of political duty, pledged itself not to interfere with religious matters, which it rightfully reserved as entirely without the bounds of its competence."[17] In an 1837 pastoral letter, the bishops argued that Catholics were free and American precisely because they need to give "no religious allegiance to any State in this Union, nor to its general government."[18] Again, de Tocqueville, who doubted that Catholics would be so zealously democratic, "if they were rich and preponderant," saw that the church's position led it to insist on the secular character of the state: "Nowhere is that doctrine of the Church which prohibits the worship reserved to God alone from being offered to the state more clearly inculcated or more generally followed."[19]

Unfortunately, the issue of Catholicism and the nation went far beyond the governmental sphere. The huge waves of immigrants who flooded the cities of the East overwhelmed the careful distinctions and cosmopolitan toleration of the early bishops and made the task of securing the church and winning respectability for it more subtle and potentially explosive. "Religion provided the necessary tradition and stability that made the democratic experiment possible. Most observers did not doubt this," according to historian Jerald C. Brauer. "The lack of inherited responsibilities, of the balance wheel of aristocracy, and of the multiform institutions of state and society had to be remedied by some force or institution in American life. Religion played that role. By removing it from political life, it could become the unitive, stable force undergirding all social life."[20] De

---

[16]William McCloskey to Martin John Spalding, 17 February 1865, quoted in Thomas W. Spalding, *Martin John Spalding: American Churchman* (Washington, 1973) 240-241.

[17]Quoted in ibid., 251.

[18]Hugh J. Nolan, ed., *Pastoral Leters of the American Hierarchy* (Huntington IN, 1971) 66.

[19]De Tocqueville, *Democracy in America,* 158.

[20]Jerald C. Brauer, "Images of Religion in America," *Church History* 2:30 (March 1961): 7.

Tocqueville made the same point when he argued that "there is no country in the world in which the Christian religion retains a greater influence over the souls of men than in America," for, while "religion in America takes no direct part in the government of society, it must be regarded as the foremost of the political institutions of the country, for if it does not impart a taste for freedom, it facilitates the use of free institutions." According to de Tocqueville, all Americans without exception regarded religion as "indispensable for the maintenance of republican institutions."[21]

Immigrant Catholicism, unlike Anglo-American Catholicism and its educated French and convert clergy, naturally appeared at first as a disruptive and divisive presence in American communities. To the economic and cultural conflicts associated with the interaction of natives and newcomers was added a discordant religious note that threatened to destroy the broad consensus many thought indispensable to social coherence and fundamental order. Anti-Catholicism always originated in this fear of disunity and division; its respectable support was always touched with anxiety about community stability.[22] The Catholic church wrestled with these problems at the pastoral level, guided by the bishops' regular affirmations of social order, hard work, and economic advancement. Immigrants themselves experienced in each generation a process of cultural disintegration and responded by building churches, schools, and charitable agencies designed to restore a semblance of order and coherence to their lives. To do so, they needed money, for there were no independent sources of revenue; both priests and lay people thus came to value respectable, ambitious families and upright, self-disciplined men and women. Community leaders, at first nervous about the Catholic presence, gradually came to appreciate the church's efforts on behalf of the poor and the workers, even while they retained a strong dislike for its faith and its organization.

Stephen Thernstrom's Newburyport, Massachussetts, for example, in 1850 had a coherent Federalist elite who looked upon Catholic immigrants and their church with fear and hostility. Slowly they learned to appreciate the church, which in Thernstrom's words organized itself under the guidance of priests and lay leaders who "were dedicated to accumulating property as well as saving souls" and who "saw clearly that a thrifty, hard working, well educated population could contribute to that end."[23]

---

[21]De Tocqueville, *Democracy in America,* 145.

[22]David Davis, "Some Themes of Countersubversion," *Mississippi Valley Historical Review* 47 (September 1960): 205-24.

[23]Stephen Thernstrom, *Poverty and Progress* (Cambridge MA, 1964) 175.

As the process of industrialization picked up after the Civil War, religious leaders such as Henry Ward Beecher argued that the task confronting the churches was to persuade men who were equal in political rights to accept the "necessary" inequality that was the inevitable result of economic laws.[24] Who could argue, then, with the Newburyport attorney who saw that, "when we pull down a Catholic Church, we must put up a penitentiary." Far better to applaud the conservative contribution of the church and welcome its shepherds into civic leadership. What Thernstrom noted of the Irish could eventually be said of most other Catholic groups: "The large, Irish Roman Catholic component of the working classes was securely attached to a church and church-related associational structure dominated by a professional and business elite committed to the prevailing American idea of success."[25]

Pressure toward conformity, arising from the needs of the wider community and the aspirations of many of its most committed and generous members, had to be balanced by the church's continuing struggle to secure the allegiance of new immigrants entering the social structure at the bottom. Equally important, the pastoral response that required national parishes, parochial schools, and ethnic organizations seemed to institutionalize social divisions and to threaten class and group conflict, thus undermining community well-being. Accordingly, with few exceptions, the bishops at once helped create a mosaic church of various nationalities and taught their members to avoid unnecessary emphasis on group interests in the wider community. Bishop England told the United States Congress that Catholics rarely voted for political candidates because they were Catholics, and he expressed his own hope that they would be politically indistinguishable from other citizens. In 1837 and again in 1840, the bishops warned the nation's Catholics to make an honest use of the ballot to "free the contamination" of excessive partisanship. They demanded that Catholics consider only their "deliberate view of what will promote your country's good."[26] Only in New York, where John Hughes occasionally mobilized Catholic voters to defend Catholic interests, was the general tone of civic harmony and political disinterest violated.

Even Hughes, however, joined other bishops in demanding law and order. Carroll had told Catholics to "conduct themselves on all occasions

---

[24]Henry May, *Protestant Churches and Industrial America* (New York, 1967) 67-72; Eric Goldman, *Rendezvous with Destiny* (New York, 1959) 71.

[25]Thernstrom, *Poverty and Progress,* 179.

[26]Nolan, *Pastoral Letters,* 60-107.

as subjects zealously attached to the government''; and in 1852, as the nation was torn by sectional divisions and intergroup tension, the bishops again adjured their people:

> Obey the public authorities. . . . Show your attachment to the institutions of our beloved country by prompt compliance with all its requirements and by the cautious jealousy with which you guard the maintenance of public authority and private rights. Thus will you refute the idle babblings of foolish men and will best prove yourselves worthy of the privileges you enjoy, and overcome by the test of practical patriotism all the prejudices which your principles but too often produce.[27]

In the same pastoral letter the bishops noted somewhat self-consciously: "Not only do we have to erect and maintain the church, the seminary and the school, but we have to fund hospitals, establish orphanages, and provide for every want of suffering humanity which religion forbids us to neglect." This work, more than any other, won respect and support for the church. The growth of such institutions at first seemed to suggest dangerous Catholic power, but later it was recognized as a major contribution to community well-being. In the late nineteenth century, James Cardinal Gibbons argued, "The more we extend the Christian religion, the more we contribute to the stability of our political and social fabric," and by that time many agreed. Indeed, Gibbons maintained that if the United States did not have "over against each other . . . hostile nationalities with different languages, different points of view, and different aspirations," it was because of the assimilating power of the church.[28] Perceptive settlement-house workers came to appreciate this, but at the same time they wondered how such separatism could be reconciled with the obvious need for united civic spirit, if the public interest was to be asserted over private group interests. The question they raised was never answered and remained to plague social reformers throughout the twentieth century.

These pastoral developments in local communities took place within a shifting pattern of cultural interaction in the nation at large. From the start, Catholic bishops followed Carroll's advice that they leave no doubts about their fidelity to the nation and its institutions. However, the patriotism of the bishops was limited and strategic, a politique of patriotism, functional to ecclesiastical stability and Catholic progress but lacking the millennial vision of America as a providential nation so common among nativists and reformers. One reason was obvious: Catholics were a minority. If there was

---

[27]Ibid., 139.

[28]James Cardinal Gibbons, *A Retrospect of Fifty Years* (Baltimore and New York, 1916) 2:213.

to be a "nation with the soul of a church," it would have little room for Catholics. A distinctive reserve thus held firm through the Civil War, when Catholic leaders on both sides supported their governments. Hughes stated the bishops' position bluntly: "Well, there is but one rule for a Catholic, wherever he finds himself, and that is to do his duty as a citizen."[29] Hughes did his by backing the North, trying to calm the draft rioters in 1863 and visiting Europe to defend the Union cause at the request of his friend, Secretary of State William Henry Seward. His path crossed that of Charleston's bishop, Patrick Lynch, who was in Europe on a similar mission for the Confederacy.

The war, meanwhile was no crusade for Catholics, North or South. Hughes showed the limits of Catholic nationalism in a letter to Secretary of War Simon Cameron: "The Catholics, so far as I know, whether of native of foreign birth, are willing to fight to the death for the support of the Constitution, the Government and the laws of the country. But if it should be understood that, with or without knowing it, they are to fight a war for the abolition of slavery, then, indeed, they will turn in disgust from the discharge of what would otherwise be a patriotic duty."[30] Like their counterparts in Europe, American bishops recognized the need to endorse the claims of the nation in times of crisis, or else to risk the allegiance of their own people and the security of their hard-won institutions, while at the same time setting limits to the nation's religious claims.

Catholics were as likely as others to interpret the war in religious terms, but they avoided the apocalyptic fervor of Protestant opinion. While they spoke of divine punishment on the nation for sins of materialism and intolerance (though not for the sin of slavery), they tended to interpret the war less in terms of the nation than in terms of the church. Drawing on a long tradition of Catholic apologetics, they argued that Protestant principles, especially private judgment, were incompatible with the order, authority, and unity necessary for civilized nations. The sectarianism and divisiveness of Protestantism, evident in the chaos of American religion and the zealotry of abolitionists, was thus a major cause of the war. Because the war so clearly illustrated the weakness of Protestantism as a religion that could unify the Republic, Catholics were inclined to be optimistic

---

[29]Quoted in Judith Conrad Wimmer, "Nation in Need of the Church: American Catholic Interpretations of the Civil War" (Ph.D. diss., Drew University, 1979) 34.

[30]Quoted in Dorothy Dohen, *Nationalism and American Catholicism* (New York, 1967) 41.

that the country would turn to the Catholic church in the aftermath of the national crisis. "The Civil War provided a tragic example of what could happen to a Republic if it continued to be guided by the divisive spirit and anti-authoritarianism of Protestantism," a recent historian notes. "The Civil War also made it possible for these ideas to receive a wider hearing than before."[31]

When bishops from North and South met in plenary council in 1866 to celebrate the successful preservation of their unity through the long, bloody war, they drew the point clearly in a pastoral letter, arguing that in "the sects the individual is the ultimate judge of what the law of God forbids and allows, and is consequently liable to claim the sanction of the higher law for what after all may be and often is but the suggestion of an undisciplined mind and overheated imagination." Such a principle undermined civil authority and opened the door to chaos and rebellion. "The Catholic, on the other hand, has a guide in the church, as a divine institution, which enables him to discriminate between what the law of God forbids and allows," and this power alone can in the long run secure the republic.[32]

The logical extension of this position was a new enthusiasm to pursue America and Americans. Isaac Hecker, founder of the Paulist Fathers, who were dedicated to the conversion of Americans to the church, expressed this hopeful sense of new opportunities in a speech to the 1866 council:

> No where is there a promise of a brighter future for the church than in our own country. Here, thanks to our American constitution, the church is free to do her divine work. Here she finds a civilization in harmony with her divine teachings. Here Christianity is promised a reception from an intelligent and free people . . . religion is never so beautiful as when in connection with knowledge and freedom. Let us therefore arise and open eyes to the bright future that is before us. Let us labor with a lively faith, a firm hope, and a charity that knows no bounds, by every good work and good example, for the reign of God's Kingdom on earth.[33]

Hecker himself enjoyed a positive response when he toured the nation, explaining Catholicism in public halls and lyceums. Priests and laypeople, especially the more educated, experienced the nationalizing effects of the war and emerged more determined to convert the country and its people. Foremost among this new breed was Archbishop John Ireland of St. Paul. He was at once Civil War chaplain, temperance reformer, inspired orator,

---

[31]Wimmer, "Nation in Need," chap. 4.

[32]Nolan, *Pastoral Letters*, 147-48.

[33]Isaac Hecker, Sermon at 1866 Council, *Hecker Papers*, Paulist Fathers Archives, New York.

and "full-blooded American." For Ireland, the war had been the "test needed to give the Republic the full consciousness of her power, and never was she so strong in the elements of life, never so entrancing in beauty, never so menacing to the foes of democracy as when the sun of Appomattox shone on her banner and revealed upon its azure ground the full galaxy of her stars."[34] Ireland for the first time among Catholics articulated the vision of special American destiny: the United States was "a providential nation" with a "divine mission . . . to prepare the world, by example and moral influence, for the universal reign of liberty and human rights." Sweeping away the careful distinctions of the older generation of bishops, Ireland seized the leadership of an emerging group of Catholics restless with the defensiveness and isolation of the past. He set before them a vision of the future in which the nation, and the Catholic church within it, would determine the fate of all humanity.

> In the course of history Providence selects now one nation now another to be the guide and the exemplar of humanity's progress. . . . A great era, the like of which has not been seen, is now dawning on the horizon. Which will now be God's chosen nation to guide the destinies of mankind? The chosen nation of the future! She is before my soul's vision. Giant in stature, bouyant in the freshness of morning youth, matronly in prudent stepping, the ethereal breezes of liberty caressing with loving touch her tresses, she is—no one seeing her can doubt it—the queen, the mistress, the teacher of coming ages. To her keeping the Creator has entrusted a mighty continent whose shores two oceans lave, rich in nature's gifts, inbosoming precious minerals, fertile in soil, salubrious in air, beauteous in vesture, the fair region of his predilection, which he had held in reserve for long centuries, awaiting the propitious moment in humanity's evolution to bestow it on men, when men were worthy to possess it. . . . Of this nation it is the mission to give forth a new humanity. She embodies in her life and her institutions the hopes, the ambitions, the dreamings of humanity's priests and prophets. To her daring in the race of progress, to her devotion at the shrine of liberty, there is no limit. Peace and prosperity spread over her their sheltering wings.
>
> The nation of the future! Need I name it? Your hearts quiver loving it.[35]

Like Hecker, Ireland saw the nation ripe for conversion, and the church's ethnocultural diversity as an obstacle to that end. "The Church will never be strong in America," he wrote, "the Church will never be sure of keeping within her fold the children of the immigrants, until she has gained a decided ascendancy among the Americans themselves." Accordingly, Catholicism must be presented in a form attractive to Americans. "The great objection which they have until now urged against her, an objection which at certain periods of her history they have entertained

---

[34]John Ireland, *The Church and Modern Society* (St. Paul, 1905) 172.
[35]Ibid., 138-39.

so strongly as to raise up persecutions against her, is that the Catholic Church is composed of foreigners, that it exists in America as an alien institution, and that it is consequently a menace to the existence of the republic."[36]

To overcome these objections and to realize the great aim of converting America, Ireland and his supporters had a program that fused an ideology of Americanism to the process of Americanization. They established a national university to focus Catholic energies on the engagement of American culture and to provide a center for mobilizing and directing national resources and raising up a generation of educated, zealous, and patriotic priests. They hoped for an accommodation with public schools to end the expense and parochialism of Catholic education. They pushed for the rapid assimilation of immigrants and resistance to ethnic movements operating under the Catholic banner, while at the same time they sought to organize lay Catholics to carry the church into the heart of national life, creating a "church of energetic individuals" participating fully in American life and bringing the Church to reconciliation with progress, liberty, and modern civilization.[37] All the while, the liberals went out of their way to proclaim their loyalty to and love for America, with Ireland again in the lead: "Believe me, no hearts love thee more ardently than Catholic hearts, no tongues speak more honestly thy praises than Catholic tongues, and no hands will be lifted up stronger and more willing to defend in war and peace thy laws and institutions than Catholic hands. *Esto Perpetua.*"[38]

Ireland was not alone; he was the leader of a party that was unwise enough to enlist Roman support for their projects, convinced that, in Bishop John Keane's words, "the Church and Democracy are fast drawing nearer" under the liberal Pope Leo XIII.[39] Unfortunately, the dreams of the liberal bishops appealed only to a small core of native-born, convert, or assimilated Irish-American priests and laypeople. European liberal Catholics, defeated in the ultramontane triumph of Vatican I, admired Ireland and took heart from the apparent emergence of a liberal church in the United States. Their support for

---

[36]Quoted in James H. Moynihan, *The Life of Archbishop Ireland* (New York, 1953) 58.

[37]Robert D. Cross, *The Emergence of Liberal Catholicism in America* (Cambridge MA, 1968).

[38]Ireland, *Modern Society*, 46-47.

[39]Keane to James Cardinal Gibbons, 31 July 1894, in P. H. Ahern, *The Catholic University of America 1887-1896: The Rectorship of John J. Keane* (Washington, 1948) 149-50.

Americanism, however, brought it under suspicion in the dominant conservative circles in Europe and in Rome. At home, their pursuit of national organization and pastoral Americanization divided the hierarchy, opened the door to a new level of Roman control, and threatened to undermine the balanced strategy of ethnocultural pluralism within the church and careful, cautious accommodation with the wider culture. New waves of immigrants from southern and eastern Europe adapted German-style forms of separate parishes and schools, while conservative bishops joined and eventually won the struggle for influence in Rome. The result was papal interventions that not only suppressed the Americanism of the liberals but ended as well the relative unity and autonomy of the American hierarchy, which had allowed it to pursue an independent course for a century.[40]

Leo XIII's position became clear in 1895, when he explained that the apostolic delegation established two years earlier was intended to implement the decrees of Vatican I and tighten up the hierarchical discipline of the church. Of course, the United States was "destined for greater things," Leo believed, and the church "should not only share in but help to bring about this prospective greatness." But she would be able to "attain these objects the more easily and abundantly in proportion to the degree in which the future shall find her constitution perfected." Each bishop was to look to the delegate and to Rome as the source and support of authority, not as in the past, to their own collegial body. To fortify the discipline of the church further, the Pope urged the bishops to encourage Catholics to organize together and not mingle too freely in the wider society. "Unless forced by necessity to do otherwise," he wrote, Catholics should "associate with Catholics." Amid the dangers posed by "familiar intercourse and intimacy between Catholics and those estranged from the Catholic name," the bishops were urged to "instruct, admonish, strengthen and urge them on to the pursuit of virtue and to the faithful observance . . . of their duties toward the church." In contrast to the enthusiastic pursuit of assimilation and penetration of secular life advocated by the liberals, Leo insisted that "this truth should sink day by day more deeply into the minds of Catholics—namely, that they can in no better way safeguard their own individual interests and the common good then by yielding in hearty submission and obedience to the Church."[41]

---

[40]See Thomas T. McAvoy, *The Great Crisis in American Catholic History* (Chicago, 1957); Gerald Fogarty, *The Vatican and the Americanist Crisis* (Rome, 1974); Robert Emmett Curran, *Michael Augustine Corrigan and the Shaping of Conservative Catholicism in America, 1878-1902* (New York, 1977).

[41]Leo XIII, "Longingua Oceani," in John Tracy Ellis, ed., *Documents in American Catholic History* (Chicago, 1967) 2:499-510.

Subsequently a dispute broke out in Europe over the meaning of Ireland's liberalism, a dispute that centered on the figure of Hecker. In 1899, Leo routed the liberals with a letter condemning a series of propositions labeled "Americanism," in which he described a tendency to minimize doctrine and the need for spiritual direction in order to win a hearing from non-Catholics. Behind the condemnation was a fear that the church in the United States might become too American. "The suspicion has arisen that there are those among you who desire a church in America different from the Church in the rest of the world." Leo reminded American Catholics that "one in the unity of doctrine as in the unity of government, such is the Catholic Church and, since God has established its center and foundation in the chair of Peter, one which is rightly called Roman, for where Peter is, there is the Church." [42]

Following hard upon the condemnation of Americanism came a series of changes that permanently altered the structure of American Catholic life. No further national councils of bishops met after 1884; when national organization reappeared in the wake of World War I, Rome insisted that the authority of the National Catholic Welfare Conference be carefully circumscribed. A "state's rights church" with each bishop supreme within his jurisdiction and accountable to no one but Rome replaced the self-consciously collegial hierarchy of the nineteenth century. Key dioceses were headed by Roman-strained bishops, selected with the help of the apostolic delegate. Surveillance committees, established in the wake of the modernist condemnation of 1905, ensured the teaching of ultramontane theology, while the lingering suspicion of Americanism kept venturesome thought under wraps. Chancery offices grew, bishops assumed closer direction of the training of priests, and vigorous newspapers were purchased by bishops or died of isolation. Catholic schools were no longer questioned, and a host of Catholic organizations and movements under clerical or episcopal direction helped maintain the unity and loyalty of Americanizing laypeople.

After the turn of the century American Catholicism thus entered its own subculture, tightly disciplined and surrounded by the structural fences of activities that limited primary associations. What had begun with Carroll and England as a careful balancing of religious loyalty with political and economic independence became in the twentieth century a rigid segregation of private and public life. By the 1920s, the bishops had become preoccupied with personal morality, family life, and an extended network

---

[42]Leo XIII, "Testem Benevolentiae," ibid., 537-46.

of parish and diocesan activities that confined personal relationships and social and cultural activity to an ethnic community or to church-related associations. Hard work in economic life and civic virtue in political life were affirmed, but in business and politics Catholics were generally left to their own devices. The unjust businessman or the corrupt politician needed fear the judgment of his church only if his activities were publicly exposed and thus threatened the respectability of his church. Otherwise the only test of his Catholicity was loyalty, measured in financial contributions, church attendance, and visible participation in Catholic organizations, and at least apparent adherence to church teachings in his marriage and family life. Catholic schools, which both measured and instilled such loyalty, along with parishes with strictly enforced liturgical rules and a host of groups and associations, cemented the subculture, whose unity, coherence, and discipline were ensured by a docile clergy carefully controlled by powerful bishops and their expanding diocesan bureaucracies. To counter potential dangers, social-action programs sought to relieve the needy, encourage conservative labor unions, and ease the adjustment of new immigrants, while foreign missions and vigorous but controlled religious orders provided safety valves for creative idealism.

Catholics remained Americans, however, and continued to require forms of engagement with the wider culture that would enhance internal morale and move the church toward acceptance and legitimacy in the wider community. To replace Protestantism as an external enemy that threatened church and society alike, Catholics discovered secularism. William Halsey's recent study of Catholic culture between the world wars traces the enthusiastic effort of Catholic intellectuals to become defenders of American innocence by joining Catholic philosophy with the values of the American genteel tradition.[43] Just when secular intellectuals, confronted with the tragic issues of the twentieth century, were moving further and further from the optimism, idealism, and civility of the nineteenth century, Catholics began to defend that latter style and claim authentic Americanism for themselves. As Michael Williams, founder of the *Commonweal,* put it in 1928: "We Catholics have all the qualifications necessary not only for successful defense of the Catholic Church but also for assuming the leadership of all other non-Catholic elements in the nation who share with Catholics a justified apprehension of the dissolving and destructive efforts of movements such as Bolshevism, Communism, and materialistic sci-

---

[43]William Halsey, *The Survival of American Innocence: Catholicism in an Era of Disillusionment* (Notre Dame, 1980).

ence."[44] Convinced that secularism endangered both religious faith and national morale, Catholics were persuaded that they could "re-Americanize America." In political theory, for example, they continued to show how Catholicism upheld order, authority, and the common good. They pointed also to its defense of social justice, all the while exposing the excessive individualism of American life. A host of Catholic intellectual and cultural organizations, movements, and publications expressed the conviction that the church had all the answers to national problems. Liberal impulses to engage the wider society and culture, combined with the isolation from modernity provided by the Catholic subculture, produced an unusual form of Catholic dissent.

Even as late as the 1950s, the Catholic world was shaken with controversy when Msgr. John Tracy Ellis lamented the generally low level of Catholic intellectual life. Ellis was upset in part because Catholic complacency prevented the church from filling the vacuum in American culture caused by the exhaustion of secular liberalism; Catholics could re-Americanize America by drawing on the resources of their tradition of Christian culture. Similarly, John Courtney Murray, whose writings on church and state led to his silencing by church authorities, believed that Catholics, almost alone, still held to the fundamental truths of the "American proposition." Therefore, they had an obligation to emerge from their subculture to show other Americans how the church alone could preserve the national consensus against corrosive secularism at home and aggressive communism abroad.

While isolating Catholics from close associations with others and denouncing a secularism they claimed pervaded public education, entertainment, and government bureaucracies, Catholic bishops had no quarrel with American institutions. Indeed they believed with the convert Frederick J. Kinsman that there was nothing in the American Constitution the church need oppose: "It is assumed that American institutions are in conformity with the law of God."[45] The bishops went further whenever national unity was seen as endangered. In World War I, they organized to support the war effort and to suppress ethnic resistance; after the war they launched Americanization programs of civic education among immigrants, and in

---

[44]Michael Williams, *The Present Position of Catholics in the United States* (New York: 1928) 12.

[45]Frederick J. Kinsman, *Catholicism and Americanism* (New York, 1924) 86.

the late 1930s, they based their isolationism on a sometimes hysterical celebration of national innocence and uniqueness.[46]

While claiming national values for themselves, however, Catholics could not claim the government, for they were still a minority, as the Al Smith campaign, prohibition, and the Spanish Civil War all demonstrated. They supported New Deal reforms but were suspicious of New Deal intentions; they affirmed patriotic nationalism but opposed internationalist foreign policy; they supported American participation in the Second World War but warned President Roosevelt of the dangers of the Soviet alliance. Churchmen first, the bishops fought for parochial schools and against aid to Franco's opponents; for public regulation of plays and films and against pornography and birth control. Defeated in 1928, they claimed to be more American than those who in effect denied their right to be Americans by imposing a religious test for office. In the 1940s, they helped organize the cold war but were divided on the peacetime draft and internal subversion. In short, Catholic nationalism waxed strong, rooted in Catholic progress and gratitude, accentuated by intergroup conflicts, and modified by church interests. It was a nationalism that saw national decline as Catholic opportunity, not to bring about reconciliation by converting people, but to enhance Catholic unity and morality by identifying the faith with traditional American values and authentic national interests.

This stance was pastorally effective because it brought church teachings in line with both religious and patriotic requirements. Nothing illustrated this harmony better than episcopal statements on the family and sexuality, justifying Catholic difference (and therefore Catholic identity), but in no way threatening the church's security or hard-won respectability. In 1949, for example, the bishops were contending that Catholic schools taught real patriotism and that the church alone was an authentic defender of democracy against communism. The gravest threat to the nation, however, was the assault of "godless philosophy" on family life: "Viewing the country and the world by and large, and noting the growing tendency to ignore God and deprive him of his rights in society, the lethal danger to the family is neither chimerical nor remote," the bishops cried. "It is a present danger, more fearsome than the atomic bomb."[47]

Catholics in the post-World War II years endorsed the national consensus around social policy and the cold war, but they argued that many

---

[46]David J. O'Brien, *American Catholics and Social Reform: The New Deal Years* (New York, 1968).

[47]Nolan, *Pastoral Letters,* 420.

others who shared in that consensus were accepting values and practices at odds with it. Murray regarded secular intellectuals as the "new barbarians," who undermined standards of judgment and corrupted the "inherited, intuitive wisdom by which the people have always lived," not by offering new beliefs but by "creating a climate of doubt and bewilderment in which clarity about the larger aims of life is dimmed and the self-confidence of the people is destroyed."[48] At the same time, Murray and other progressive Catholics were impatient with a Catholicism that refused to take up the challenge to re-Americanize America. They continued to feel cut off from the nation by the Catholic subculture, and they chafed at points of view that seemed to serve less as challenges to bring the church into the arena to win over the nation than as balm for Catholic morale.

The new generation of Catholic reformers no longer saw any need to distance themselves from American culture. Protestantism was too weak and divided to pose a danger, while secular liberalism had been placed on the defensive by the tragedies of the war and had been discredited, in their view, by its association with communism. In the writings of the new conservatives of the 1950s, Catholic liberals found evidence of a need for the certainty and assurance that Catholicism alone could supply. The church, for its part, had emerged from the war stronger than ever. The papacy was a respected symbol of resistance to communism, and Christian Democratic governments were leading the reconstruction of western Europe. In the United States the Catholic population was expanding rapidly, while educational opportunities available through the GI Bill of Rights were easing Catholic ascent in politics, the professions, and business. Religious vocations, school enrollments, and building programs were at an all-time high—evidence enough that American institutions were sound. Catholics had never doubted that national ideas were valid; to assure a peculiarly American and democratic form of reconquest, they needed only to end Catholic aloofness and to strive energetically to engage the problems and possibilities of American society.

Conservative Catholics, convinced that a degree of alienation was necessary to the unity and coherence of the church, resisted reform efforts until Vatican II undercut their position. In a very short time, the foundations of the Catholic subculture collapsed, and when they did, the careful balancing of national and ecclesiastical loyalties no longer seemed appropriate. Instead, the renewal of the church and creative participation in American culture now seemed to go hand in hand. The early commenta-

---

[48]John Courtney Murray, *We Hold These Truths* (New York, 1960) 41, 43.

tors on the council, John Cogley, Michael Novak, and Daniel Callahan, seemed to value renewal precisely because it would facilitate that participation. American culture would supply new symbols for liturgical celebration, new models for church organization, new opportunities for apostolic service. Opening itself to the American experience, affirming its own newly educated, middle-class laity, and being less preoccupied with its own agenda, the church would become more energetic and more free, committing itself to the goals and values of a progressive, democratic America, itself in need of people of faith and wisdom. Emerging from the ghetto, the church would encourage its members to join actively with other persons of good will to solve the problems of American society and to build a more just and peaceful world.[49]

Things did not work out as expected, and the present confusion in Catholic ranks derives from the convergence in the 1960s of three strands of change. The sociological cement of the American church, its status as an immigrant, working-class, minority faith, was transformed by the social changes of the postwar years, so that, if there had never been a council, there would still have been enormous pressure for change. There was a council, which opened up the understanding of what the church is and what its mission should be in the world. Together these resulted in a new voluntarism, a new sense that people can and will choose for themselves both their religious affiliation and the terms of that belonging. While all this change was going on, the nation itself experienced profound shocks, making the decade a decisive break in American religious history, according to historian Sydney Ahlstrom. Catholics who had long desired to bring the church to the center of American life discovered, like Daniel Berrigan, that the taste could turn bitter or, with Monsignor Geno Baroni, that the journey that began in an Italian-American kitchen had ended at McDonald's, and they wondered whether the trip was worth the struggle.

Even the bishops, long willing to claim American symbols when helpful but mainly concerned with the vitality and strength of the church, faced far deeper problems when they confronted racism, poverty, and war. In 1971, the United States bishops became the first hierarchy in modern times to judge their nation's conduct unjust in the middle of a war.[50] As Catho-

---

[49]David J. O'Brien, *The Renewal of American Catholicism* (New York, 1972) chaps. 4-5.

[50]David J. O'Brien, "American Catholic Opposition to the Vietnam War: A Preliminary Assessment," in Thomas A. Shannon, ed., *War or Peace? The Search for New Answers* (Maryknoll NY, 1980) 119-51.

lics entered the mainstream, there to confront the profound shocks of modern consciousness, the Catholic subculture seemed to collapse behind them. As their confidence in their ability to lead or to convert the nation waned, they were no longer sure where to go. A few old-time conservatives such as Cardinal Krol continued to worry about a secularism that threatened both the nation and the church, but most Catholic leaders thought that the problem went deeper than that. While few went as far as the seeming anti-Americanism of such highly visible church activists as Berrigan, many did feel that the church had been damaged by too intimate an identification with national values and civic symbols.

Historian Philip Gleason provided one thoughtful analysis of Catholic experience in 1969 under the heading "The Crisis of Americanization."[51] Gleason argued convincingly that the changes in American Catholicism in the 1960s amounted to a natural and generally beneficial adjustment to the growing Americanization of the Catholic population. The church itself could be seen as an "institutional immigrant," Gleason argued: it constantly changed to meet the requirements of a shifting American environment and a variable Catholic population, but not changing so much as to lose its distinctive identity. A few years later, however, Gleason became convinced that the church had gone too far in this process of accommodation. Frenzied agitation and utopian expectations had brought about not Americanization but disintegration. Citing John Tracy Ellis's "sad acknowledgement that some Catholics had all but surrendered to a humanist creed," Gleason expressed the mood of Catholic liberals after a decade of reform: "The strongest sense I had was of a church, a religious tradition that was coming undone, breaking apart, losing its coherence."[52] Wilfred Sheed, Garry Wills, and James Hitchcock, ideologically dissimilar as they appear, all shared this feeling of collapse and absorption of Catholicism into the tragically disrupting currents of the country at large.

As a result of the failure of liberal reforms, some Catholics have now become increasingly attracted to basically sectarian approaches to renewal, which would put a new distance between the church and American culture. This stance arises less from realistic assessment of the problems and possibilities of the church than from disillusionment with modern culture. At the beginning of the process of renewal, Karl Rahner said that the

---

[51]Philip Gleason, "The Crisis of Americanization," in Philip Gleason, ed., *Contemporary Catholicism in the United States* (Notre Dame, 1969) 32-33.

[52]Philip Gleason, "In Search of Unity: American Catholic Thought, 1920-1960," *Catholic Historical Review* 65 (April 1979): 185-205.

church of the future would be marked by faith's becoming a matter of "personal decision constantly renewed amid perilous surroundings." Rahner continues to insist that the faith decision will be made in "perilous surroundings": the church of the future, he argues, will be "made up of those who have struggled against the environment in order to reach a personally clear and explicitly responsible decision of faith." Gathered together like a "deviant minority," Rahner's church will become, in his own words, "sociologically speaking, sectarian."[53]

American theologian Avery Dulles shares Rahner's pessimism. The Christianity of the future, he writes, "will be a stance of committed individuals who are personally strong enough to stand up against the prevalent assumptions of the civilization in which they find themselves." Dulles thinks that the future will be marked by "paganism," so that "Christians who wish to retain any firm beliefs or adhere to any moral norms will have to distance themselves from the dominant culture . . . which will go its own way without being greatly influenced by the church."[54] Reformers such as Dulles and Rahner thus join the conservatives in turning away from what one Roman cardinal called "the absurd pretension of improving the world," and they might even find themselves sympathethic to Malcolm Muggeridge, who blames the church's troubles on its "succumbing to the siren voice of material and fleshly well being wafted across the Atlantic."

Pope John XXIII and Vatican II had seemed to suggest that the church would come into the midst of life, accepting a role in which the world's problems are the church's problems, the world's destiny the church's own. As Vatican II proclaimed: "The joys and hopes, the griefs and anxieties of the men of this age, especially those who are poor or in any way afflicted, these too are the joys and hopes, the griefs and anxieties of the followers of Christ."[55] Even then, perceptive observers feared that the church, which, by struggling against perceived enemies such as Protestants, secularists, and communists, had found the boundaries of identity and energy for commitment, would not be able to maintain a position in which it accepted responsibility for the world and sought to minister to people from within the contours of human culture. For American Catholics, the effort to do so meant either an absorption into a secular society still profoundly

---

[53]Karl Rahner, *The Shape of the Church to Come* (New York, 1974) 74.

[54]Avery Dulles, *The Resilient Church* (New York: 1977) 21.

[55]"The Pastoral Constitution on the Church in the Modern World," in David J. O'Brien and Thomas A. Shannon, eds., *Renewing the Earth: Catholic Documents on Peace, Justice, and Liberation* (New York, 1977) 178.

anti-Catholic, as conservatives and radicals believe, or the weakening of the distinctive identity that alone can ground allegiance, organization, and commitments, as church leaders indifferent to ideology discover.

The combination of social change within the Catholic community itself and the shifts in perceptions of the church and its mission occasioned by the council resulted in a long-delayed confrontation between Catholicism and modern culture. In the United States that confrontation was made particularly agonizing by the isolation from modern life long fostered by the powerful subculture in which midcentury Catholics had been nurtured. They retained an innocence about the country, and more profoundly about politics and power, that virtually ensured a degree of disappointment. The events of the sixties accentuated the extremes of high hopes and bitter disillusionment, and when Catholics looked back to the church from which they had "emerged," it seemed disorganized, unsure of itself, lacking the remembered assurance and certainty—which, it turned out, had been rooted less in spiritual experience than in sociological isolation and organizational discipline. The result was uncertain leadership among both bishops and intellectuals, bitter internal disputes over policy among the church's professional cadres, and, for the laity and rank-and-file clergy and religious, a personal search for meaning and purpose. This search occurred in small communities based on shared experiences, in enthusiastic spiritual movements marked by ecstatic discoveries of Jesus, in programs of renewal in parishes and religious communities based on personal decisions about faith; it all marked an erosion of the cultural power of Catholicism, both within its own ranks and in the nation at large.

The most significant casualty of the encounter of church and culture is Catholic liberalism. Few serious Catholics are any longer interested in exploring the distinctively American quality of the church in the United States; few seem to offer, or possess, a vision of a unique role for the American church in the larger world. Liberal Catholics loved the nation too much and have been disappointed; conservatives loved it too little and are not surprised. Each side chooses to separate itself from the nation, in biblical prophecy on the left or ghetto isolation on the right. Understandable as such positions may be in light of religious and cultural imperatives, they constitute forms of civic corruption that, in Robert Bellah's terms, places one's own good, even that of the church, before the common good; love of self, even of one's own integrity, before love of the neighbor. Bellah quotes Montesquieu: "A republic will survive only so long as its citizens love it." Church leaders easily denounce selfishness as a matter of civic concern, but rarely do they admit that it marks voluntary associations, even churches, as well as individuals.[56] Must one love church before nation, or was Pope John XXIII right when he said that the time had come "to defend above all and everywhere the rights of the human person and not just those of the Catholic church?"[57] To choose a merely personal understanding of Christian faith, defined in opposition to and in judgment on American culture, or to choose a merely Catholic understanding of church and mission, indifferent to the nation and its people, equally endangers the Republic by withdrawing from its public life a community that champions freedom, justice, and peace as values that, although transcending the nation, alone give the nation hope that its failures may be redeemed and its possibilities realized.[58]

Here, as in so many cases, the Catholic problem merges with that of the larger Christian community in the United States. Robert Handy once described the period from 1925 to 1935 as "the American religious depression," when mainline Protestantism, which had deeply identified with American culture, was overwhelmed by disillusionment. Beset by internal conflicts and declining self-confidence, the Protestant churches suffered sharp drops in church attendance, Sunday school enrollments, budgets, and social programs. Its two dominant ideologies were discredited: fundamentalism, by its association with prohibition, the Klan, and the Scopes trial; modernism, by its gradual surrender to secular humanism. "While liberals were fighting off the frontal attack of the fundamentalists," Handy wrote, "they were inadvertently backing toward the humanist position."[59] Not only could secular advocates of humanism claim to speak more authentically to a "scientifically and naturalistically inclined age," but when the brutality and cynicism of the thirties became evident, liberal idealism and optimism had little to say. Equally important, liberalism, by its accommodation to culture, ended by having no solid answer to the question, "Why the church?"

According to Handy, "inner change" was needed if Protestantism was to deal with the needs of the time in a fresh and creative way. In particular, the church needed to recover its own standpoint and uniqueness if it was

---

[56]Robert Bellah, "The Role of Preaching in a Corrupt Republic," *Christianity and Crisis* (25 December 1978): 317-22.

[57]Giancarlo Zizola, *The Utopia of Pope John XXIII* (Maryknoll NY, 1978) 246.

[58]Peter Berger, "Catholic Presence in America," *Origins* (6 May 1976): 725-28.

[59]Robert T. Handy, "The American Religious Depression, 1925-35," *Church History* 29 (January 1960): 3-16.

to have confidence in its ability to critique and contribute to the world around it. Under the leadership of Reinhold Niebuhr, Protestantism gradually did recover a distinctively Christian belief and witness that did not require a rejection of critical scholarship or social responsibility. Those who guided Protestant theology to the right, toward orthodoxy, also contributed to a vigorous renewal of social criticism and social action. They were able to do so because, unlike neoorthodox leaders of Europe, they continued to believe in the possibility of social reform in the United States; they had not lost faith in the nation or its people. Mainline Protestantism remained committed to the search for social justice, civil rights, and world peace during the postwar reaction, the conflicts of the sixties, and the resurgent complacency of the seventies. As William Hutchinson has argued, neoorthodoxy modified but did not displace the liberal Protestant determination to live at the intersection of faith and culture, whatever the uncertainties or ambiguities such a life required.[60]

The parallels with recent Catholic history are striking. Liberalism, too quick to accommodate to American society, was compromised when that society revealed its flaws. Ireland's hysterical nationalism could not withstand ecclesiastical counterattack, while the self-righteous aloofness and isolation of interwar culture was made possible only by refusing to face the tragic realities of modern history. Liberals of the conciliar years saw America as fundamentally good, a standpoint given flesh by the cold war and by their own experience of economic, social, and cultural advance in the postwar years. The shocks of poverty, injustice, and violence hit them the way they hit Jane Addams, Frederick C. Howe, Walter Rauschenbusch, and a generation of Protestant Social Gospel leaders when they discovered the industrial city before World War I. Both Social Gospel leaders and Catholic activists had depended on assumptions of American exceptionalism and historical benevolence, and both groups fell into the trap of cultural accommodation. They failed to distinguish between a theological and pastoral approach that takes seriously the experience of people and one that makes such experience normative for the faith and life of the church.

Although American Catholic liberalism remains naive and too ready to rely upon secular social science as a reliable guide to Christian judgment and action, it should not be rejected. A ''course correction'' is needed, however, namely, a recovery of critical distance. American Catholicism must reject a conservatism of Catholic power and doctrinal orthodoxy that

---

[60]William R. Hutchinson, *The Modernist Impulse in American Protestantism* (New York, 1979) 288-313.

ignores both the sociological reality of voluntarism and the theological identification of Christian faith with human dignity, which marks the encyclicals of John Paul II. It needs to reject with equal clarity a sectarian withdrawal to a mountaintop of biblical prophecy from which the church may hurl down its thunderbolts upon a world, a nation, and a people it has abandoned, whether under the auspices of charismatic enthusiasm or supposed dedication to peace and the poor. Rather, the church must work to recover a sense of mission, inspired by contemporary church teaching and the magnificent emergence of sister churches around the world, and rendered operative by close attention to the specifically American character of its own situation. This means probing the depths of the American experience, including the American experience of its own people. It means reexamining such issues as parish development; the role of the laity, the church, and politics; and the need for a pastoral planning that enlists the voluntary dedication of Catholics themselves.

Previous generations of Catholics have had to find their own mediating role between faith and culture in the United States, and it can be done again in ways appropriate to a church and a nation badly in need of a renewal of enthusiasm and dedication. Nailing jelly to the wall it may be, but critical reflection on civil religion and thoughtful, modest efforts to recover something of the democratic faith and the providential sense of mission that has always been central to American experience remain the unfinished agenda of Catholic renewal in the 1980s.

THE SEPARATION OF STATE AND CHURCH AND THE RISE OF CIVIL RELIGION: A JEWISH PERSPECTIVE

Manfred H. Vogel

This chapter delineates the position that Jewry and Judaism take (or ought to take) with regard to the issue of the separation of state and church and to that of civil religion. We should keep in mind, however, that these issues denote a complex of different possible situations rather than a clear-cut single phenomenon. It may be helpful, therefore, by way of introduction, to sort out briefly the main possible significations implicated in these notions.

There is no escaping the fact that the notion of the separation of state and church is ambivalent. In its most minimal signification, the notion may merely mean the disestablishment of religion; namely, it may merely denote (1) that religion is not at the service of the state, is not an office or an arm of the state, being privileged and supported by it, (2) that the state is not under the control of religion, that is, the state is not a hierocracy. As such, this signification impinges exclusively on the institutional aspect of the relation between state and religion, on the status of the institution of religion within the state. It negates any special recognition or support that the state may accord to it or, conversely, any power that it may exercise

over the state. It does not impinge, let it be noted, on the involvement of
religion within such domains of the public-national life as the social, economic, or political domains—that is, within what we may term the "horizontal dimension" of life.

Precisely with respect to the involvement of religion within horizontal
dimension, however, other possible significations may arise. The separation of state and church may well signify not only the disestablishment
of religion but furthermore the exclusion of religion from the horizontal
dimension. This latter aspect in turn may signify the total exclusion of religion from the horizontal dimension, leaving that domain exclusively at
the disposal of the state. It would thus erect a "wall of separation" between religion and the horizontal dimension—between church and state.
Clearly, this position presents the most radical signification of the notion.

On the other hand, the notion may signify only a partial exclusion of
religion from the horizontal dimension. As such, this signification would
merely draw a "line of division" between those domains upon which religion may impinge (thus sharing involvement with the state) and the other
domains from which it is excluded (thus relegating them to the sole concern of the state). This signification is clearly much less radical. It occu-
pies, so to speak, a middle ground between the minimal signification of
the "disestablishment" formulation and the maximal signification of the
"wall of separation" formulation. Furthermore, in contradistinction to
these alternative significations, it is rather elastic—it allows a great variety
of formulations, seeing that the line of division can be drawn at different
points throughout the spectrum of possibilities from the point where religion is excluded from almost all domains to the point where it is hardly
excluded from any domain of the horizontal dimension. The notion of the
separation of state and church thus implicates three distinct and different
significations, which we will have to bear in mind in our analysis below.[1]

Proceeding to the notion of civil religion, one would have to say that
it is not so much ambivalent as it is amorphous. Indeed, it can be more
readily delineated by what it is not than by what it is—it is not any of the
traditional religions. And yet, it carries features and fulfills roles that are
commonly associated with traditional religions (hence the reference to it
as a religion). It may thus include an ideological stance or display a structure of rituals. Most significantly, however, it acts as a cohesive force within

---

[1]These distinctions and indeed the characterizations of "wall of separation" and
"line of division" are derived from John F. Wilson's perceptive and judicious book
Public Religion in American Culture (Philadelphia: Temple University Press,
1979).

the community, giving it orientation, meaning, and justification. With respect to content or form, delineation of the notion may well be hopeless, since its signification may vary all the way from watered-down versions of traditional religions to neopagan versions of nationalist cults to a current secular weltanschauung (for example, democracy or communism). Still, although in the context of this paper the notion will indeed be grasped in terms of its social function (I take the notion of civil religion to signify the body of ideas, goals, customs, and ceremonies that takes the place and fulfills the functions of traditional religion within the horizontal dimension of life), it will be important to keep in mind the various possible significations of the notion as regards its content and form, for precisely these significations will prove most pertinent to the analysis below.

Although, according to our delineation here, the notion of the separation of state and church and that of the rise of civil religion are clearly separate and distinct notions, they are nonetheless intimately interlinked. The rise of civil religion necessarily presupposes the separation of state and church, since in order for a civil religion to arise, a religious vacuum must be present in the horizontal dimension (otherwise, the traditional religion would function as the civil religion, thus preempting the need or the possibility for what was delineated above as civil religion to arise). Such a religious vacuum can, in turn, be effected only through the separation of state and church. Thus, outside the context of the separation of state and church, the rise of civil religion would not be possible.

The link between the two notions, however, is even more intimate. Not only does the rise of civil religion necessarily presuppose the separation of state and church, but the *kind* of civil religion that is likely to arise will depend on the *degree* of separation existing between state and church. That is, the nature of civil religion in a given society will depend on the extent to which the traditional religion is excluded from the horizontal dimension, on whether the "wall of separation" alternative or the "line of division" alternative prevails (and in the case of the latter, on where the line is actually drawn). I would thus suggest that the less radical the exclusion of the traditional religion from the horizontal dimension is, the more likely it is that the civil religion, which may nonetheless arise in these circumstances, will fashion itself according to the traditional religion and become a watered-down version of it. On the other hand, the more radical the exclusion is, the more likely it is that the civil religion arising in these circumstances will fashion itself according to the secular and profane dimensions of the national ethos.

Because of this linkage between the two notions, any analysis of one of these notions will necessarily implicate the other also. For, as we have seen, civil religion is, in an important sense, a consequence of the separation of state and church and is indeed determined by it. Thus, one cannot really deal with the notion of the separation of state and church without weighing its consequence, namely, civil religion; conversely, one cannot really deal with the notion of civil religion without implicating that which brings it about, namely, the separation of state and church. Indeed, the analysis of one of the notions should lead to insight regarding the other notion.

Finally, we should note that the following analysis is predicated on the issues before us arising in the context of a homogeneous rather than a pluralistic nation. The results of the analysis thus cannot be applied without considerable further modifications to the situation prevailing in a pluralistic nation.

Many will therefore no doubt object that my analysis has no relevance to the situation prevailing in the United States, which many would claim is a nation that by its very makeup is pluralistic. Of course, if this claim is valid, then the point of my analysis would be greatly diminished. For there is no denying that the issues of the separation of state and church and of civil religion arise most poignantly in the context of the United States.

I am not really convinced, however, that the American nation is by its very makeup pluralistic. At the present moment (and, no doubt, for yet a number of years to come) one does indeed encounter on the American scene a pluralistic society. After all, the American nation is still a nation in the making, a nation of immigrants, and is such it is inescapably pluralistic. But this fact does not imply that the American nation is by its very makeup and thus permanently constituted as a pluralistic nation. It would be a bad mistake, in my judgment, to take the present situation as reflecting a permanent state of affairs. The present situation is but a stage in the process of the formation of a new ethnic-national entity. When this process finally crystallizes itself into a completed, finished product, I believe that the American nation, like all other ethnic-national entities, will not be pluralistic. My analysis should therefore remain relevant also for the situation in the United States, even though it deals with a homogeneous rather than a pluralistic nation. As regards the projected final state of affairs, my comments should remain relevant, explicitly so. Regarding the present, transitory state of affairs, however, they should remain implicitly relevant. For, in the last analysis, only in the light of the final state of affairs can an enlightened and valid policy be formulated for the transitory stage.

In any event, if one wishes to examine the problematic presented by the issues before us at its deepest and most challenging level, (that is, in terms of its theological implications), one must examine it in the context of a homogeneous nation. For in the context of a pluralistic nation, the theological implications are inevitably suppressed and obscured by purely pragmatic considerations. Indeed, in the light of such considerations operating in the context of a pluralistic nation, the case for the separation of state and church and for civil religion is practically made before one starts. Still, from the perspective of religion the issues do present serious theological problems, which can be seen precisely when examining the issues in the context of a homogeneous nation.

I

There can be little hesitation in stating that the preponderant majority of Jewry today (specifically of American Jewry) staunchly supports the principle that state and church should be kept completely separated.[2] Indeed, one can almost say that to oppose this principle or even merely to raise questions or qualifications with respect to its validity would be deemed in many a Jewish quarter as tantamount to being un-Jewish (let alone un-American)—to committing an act of outright betrayal of the position of Judaism or, at the very least, an act grievously detrimental to its interest.[3] As regards the issue of civil religion, we may surmise that a considerable number of Jews would prefer not to have it emerge at all and that, certainly, a preponderant majority of Jewry would prefer that it reflect as little as possible of the particularity and specificity of the traditional religion of the host nation. The less the traditional religion injects its specific doctrinal and symbolic paraphernalia into the civil religion, the more accepting will the attitude of Jewry be.

---

[2]Since, as we have noted, it is mainly in the United States that the issues of the separation of state and church and of civil religion arise most poignantly, it is inevitable that an analysis of the stance taken by Jewry vis-à-vis these issues should draw its data primarily from the position taken by American Jewry. As will become clear in the course of our analysis below, however, with regard to these issues American Jewry really depicts the position of a predominant segment of diaspora Jewry worldwide, and consequently one can legitimately speak without further qualifications of the position of Jewry in modern times.

[3]There are, however, indications that of late this position has been undergoing reexamination in some quarters of the community. In part, this shift may be due to purely utilitarian-pragmatic considerations brought about by new institutional vested interest (e.g., the desire to receive governmental support for religious day-schools). But also, and much more laudably, it may be due to a growing appreciation of the role of religion in the sociopolitical domain, on the one hand, and of the threat to Judaism that secularism may present, on the other. Indeed this chapter may be seen as reflecting this trend of thought.

It is quite understandable that a preponderant majority of Jewry should take this position, given the Jewish experience during the past two millennia of diaspora existence, when state and church were intimately united. Given the persecution and discrimination that Jews suffered during this period at the hands of the religion of the host nations when that religion (whether Christianity or Islam) did impinge on the horizontal dimension of life and had the power of the state at its disposal, it is readily understandable that Jews would wish, almost instinctively, to separate the religion of the host nation from the horizontal dimension and from the power of the state. Indeed, the long history of suffering at the hands of host religions has psychologically conditioned the Jews to favor the separation of state and church.

Beyond the matter of psychological conditioning, the position of the Jew in favor of separating state and church has also sound logic on its side. Realizing that we live in premessianic times and in a not-yet-redeemed world, one should not expect the disappearance of all rivalry and denigration among competing religions; the existence of friction—sometimes more, sometimes less, but always some friction—between different institutionalized religions is inescapable. It is clear, therefore, that by removing the host religion from the horizontal dimension and by depriving it of the power that is at the disposal of the state, one can at least minimize the threat that this friction would express itself in concrete physical action.[4] Given the conditions of diaspora existence, it is thus historically, psychologically, and logically understandable that the Jew would favor the separation of state and church.

Aside from these pervasive though somewhat diffuse considerations, we must take into account yet another aspect that is much more immediate and specific, and that explains the preponderant support by Jewry for the separation of state and church. This consideration is derived from the dynamics operating in the process of the emancipation, one that has radically transformed the conditions of Jewish existence in modern times.

The emancipation, by essentially signifying the *entry* of the Jew into the life-stream of the host nation, necessarily implicates the *assimilation* of the Jew into the host nation. The more emancipated that Jews desired to be, the more assimilated they had to become. Indeed, the early propo-

---

[4]Of course, I do not say that the religion of the host nation is necessarily deprived in this context of all special power and is thus placed on an equal footing with the other religions that may be present. On the contrary, it may still retain pervasive power by virtue of its being the religion of the majority. When separated from the state, however, it is deprived of overt and direct power.

nents of the emancipation (who, interestingly enough, came from the host nation) made the point only too clearly.[5] Emancipation was offered to Jews only qua human beings, as members of the human species, but not to Jews qua Jews, as members of a religious-national community. Jews were to be allowed to enter and share in the life of the host nation only on the clear condition that they leave their Jewishness behind—to the Jew as man, everything; to the Jew as Jew, nothing.[6] The Jew was thus to be emancipated only at the price of being "neutralized" of his or her Jewishness and fully assimilated into the ethos of the host nation.

This requirement for full assimilation would clearly necessitate, in the last analysis, embracing the religion of the host nation. Jews could fully assimilate themselves in the language, culture, mannerisms, customs, and professions of the host nation, and yet, inasmuch as they had not also embraced the religion of the host nation, their assimilation would not be complete and they would inevitably be marked as still outsiders. It is thus quite understandable that many emancipated Jews would come to see in the religion of the host nation a barrier to their full emancipation.[8]

Given the fervent desire and need of the modern Jew to be fully emancipated, there are really only two alternatives. On the one hand, the emancipated Jew could pursue his or her assimilation all the way and embrace the religion of the host nation. Many an emancipated Jew indeed took this path (clearly converting for the sake of convenience rather than out of conviction), in the belief that this action would now allow full admission into the life-stream of the host nation. As Heine said, "The baptismal certificate is the ticket of admission to European culture."[9] Many emancipated

---

[5]See, for example, the position taken by Count Clermont-Tonnere, Robespierre, Count Mirabeau, Dohm, and Herder.

[6]As Count Clermont-Tonnere put it, "The Jews should be denied everything as a nation, but granted everything as individuals," quoted in *The Jew in the Modern World,* P. Mendes-Flohr and J. Reinharz (New York: Oxford University Press, 1980) 104.

[7]For a fuller analysis of the problematic that the emancipation presents to the Jew and to Judaism, see my article "The Dilemma of Identity for the Emancipated Jew," reprinted in Martin E. Marty and Dean G. Peerman, eds. *New Theology* 4 (New York: Macmillan, 1967).

[8]Indeed, this limitation was already seen very early in the process of the emancipation. See, for example, the open letter sent by David Friedlaender to the Protestant minister W. A. Teller, quoted in Mendes-Flohr and Reinharz, *Jew,* 95-99.

[9]Ibid., 223.

Jews, however, while desiring and needing full emancipation, could not and would not take up the alternative of conversion. After all, there can be no denying that such an act signifies a most fundamental betrayal of one's deepest identity, a most radical severance of the ties to one's past and immediate environment.

These emancipated Jews (and for all intents and purposes only they constituted emancipated Jewry, since the other emancipated Jews opted out of Judaism in the act of conversion, even though halakically they may still be considered Jews) grasped at the second alternative, namely, at the exclusion of the host religion from the public life-stream of the host nation. For in such exclusion the barrier constituted by the host religion was clearly removed. Indeed, the public life-stream of the host nation now became neutralized of any and all religious considerations; it became, so to speak, a no-man's-land as far as the religious dimension was concerned. In light of our analysis here, this arrangement should have suited the emancipated Jews very nicely. For now, they did not have to pay the price of conversion in order to solve the problem of their full integration; rather, the problem was solved by removing the religious barrier. Rather than their having to adapt to the situation, the situation was adapted to their needs, since the public life-stream where their integration took place was cleared of the problematic connected with the religious dimension.[10]

This rationale, which accounts for the stance taken by emancipated Jews in favor of the separation of state and church, also accounts for their stance toward civil religion. Inasmuch as religion in general is viewed as a divisive and excluding factor, and seeing that the very aspiration of the emancipated Jew is to overcome exclusion, it is understandable that the

---

[10]The religious dimension can, of course, continue to operate in this context as long as it is confined to being a private and inward affair of the individual. In other words, the religious dimension may still function as a divisive factor, albeit not formally as a stated public policy that continues to impose disabilities upon the emancipation of the Jew. Indeed, in view of this it is understandable that many emancipated Jews are drawn to a more sweeping secularism that wishes to eradicate religion altogether, not only from the public domain but from the private domain as well. They come to hate religion generally with a vengeance, seeing it as a pernicious, divisive factor that can lead only to discrimination and discord. Still, interestingly enough, this general hatred is focused in particular against their own religion (i.e., against Judaism); after all, Judaism does not only share, qua religion, in the guilt of religion generally for introducing discrimination and hatred, but, given the circumstances of Jewish existence (i.e., the circumstances of diaspora existence), it is responsible for making them victims rather than the perpetrators of such discrimination and hatred.

emancipated Jew would prefer to have all religion eliminated from the public life-stream of the host nation.

Still, inasmuch as it is specifically the religion of the host nation that differentiates emancipated Jews and precludes their full entry into the life-stream of the host nation, it is understandable that, where the rise of a civil religion is inevitable, they would prefer that it incorporate as little as possible of the host religion. For the more removed the civil religion is from the religion of the host nation, the more equalized is the position of emancipated Jews to that of the host nation with respect to the religious factor and, consequently, the more neutralized does the obstructive aspect of the religious factor become. Of course, if the civil religion under these circumstances also incorporated some elements of their own religious heritage (and the more, the better), it would be even more congenial. Basically, however, the less the civil religion incorporates historical and doctrinal concreteness and specificity—or, in other words, the more abstract and universal it is—the less it obstructs the entry of the emancipated Jew into the life-stream of the host nation, and consequently the more congenial it becomes for the emancipated Jew to support it. The position of emancipated Jews vis-à-vis the issue of separation of state and church is thus to be understood on the basis of their perception of religion generally, and more specifically of the religion of the host nation as a divisive and excluding factor that serves to restrict their full entry into the life-stream of the host nation.

II

The position of the emancipated Jew as regards the issues of the separation of state and church and of civil religion cannot be automatically assumed to represent also the position of Judaism with regard to these issues. Certainly, the rationale operating in the case of Judaism is different from the rationale considered above, which reflects the thought of emancipated Jewry. While the latter was determined by the desires and interests of the emancipated Jew, the former must be determined by the requirements and dictates of the structure of the faith of Judaism. It is by no means the case that the interests and desires of the emancipated Jew or, for that matter, of the Jew generally do always coincide with the requirements of Jewish faith. It is ironic that the two often clash—what is good for the Jews is not necessarily good for Judaism and vice versa. With regard to the issues before us, we certainly cannot take for granted that the two positions are necessarily identical.

Indeed, if we examine the structure of Judaism's faith, we will see that its inner logic dictates a position toward the issues of the separation of state and church and of civil religion that is diametrically opposed to the position taken by the emancipated Jew. Space does not allow me to present in detail the argument for this claim, but the crux of the matter lies in the fact that mainstream Judaism necessarily requires that it have available to itself the social, economic, and ideally, also the political domains of life; namely, it requires what we have called the horizontal dimension of life. This requirement follows from the fact that, through the full gamut of human relations (including the social, the economic, and the political), mainstream Judaism responds and witnesses to the divine. The axis of the human-divine relation (the most essential aspect of any structure of faith) is essentially established here through the horizontal dimension, thus constituting the latter as the inescapable matrix through which mainstream Judaism must express itself. It clearly excludes the alternative of relegating mainstream Judaism to an exclusive concern with what we may term the vertical dimension, namely, the direct, inward relation of the individual believer to the divine, which thus separates and removes the religious concern from the horizontal dimension of life. In mainstream Judaism the religious concern, the relation to the divine, must be mediated through the horizontal dimension; it is therefore no exaggeration to say that, without the availability to itself of this latter dimension, mainstream Judaism could not function and would disintegrate.[11]

The inner logic of faith of mainstream Judaism should thus dictate opposition to the separation of state and church when it signifies the exclusion of religion from the horizontal dimension. It should require a more strenuous opposition to the "wall of of separation" alternative than to the "line of division" alternative, while within the latter approach it would show increased opposition as the line is drawn less and less in favor of religion. For clearly the separation of state and church in the context of these significations would deprive Judaism of the availability of the horizontal dimension. Since the structure of faith of mainstream Judaism requires the availability of the horizontal dimension and must opt to preserve it as much as possible, the rationale for dictating the stance delineated here is evident. Similarly, the inner logic of mainstream Judaism should dictate opposition to the rise of civil religion, though in the context where civil religion does arise, the closer it is to Judaism, the more acceptable it should be. Mainstream Judaism requires the horizontal dimension, which is tantamount to

---

[11]This point has been made by a number of people. For an excellent analysis of the link between the need of Judaism for the horizontal dimension and the problematic precipitated by the emancipation, see Max Wiener, *Judische Religion in Zeitalter der Emancipation.*

saying that mainstream Judaism perceives its own vocation to be precisely that of a civil religion. It itself should fulfill the function of civil religion, and consequently it must oppose any other formulation that would supplant it in this function.

As such, of course, the stance that the faith of mainstream Judaism dictates is diametrically opposed to the stance taken by emancipated Jewry. The latter supports the separation of state and church—lending its strongest support to the "wall of separation" alternative rather than the "line of division" alternative. As regards the rise of civil religion, though it may prefer, in the last analysis, its exclusion (thus seemingly agreeing in this instance with the stance dictated by mainstream Judaism), in the context where it does arise, the less the civil religion reflects the traditional religion, the stronger is its support for it.[12] This diametric opposition, however, between the stance taken by emancipated Jewry and the stance dictated by mainstream Judaism should not really be surprising. Indeed, it is to be expected, since, while the inner logic operating in terms of the interests of the emancipated Jew is determined by the desire to *exclude* religion from the horizontal dimension, the inner logic operating in terms of the structure of faith of mainstream Judaism is determined by the need to *include* religion within the horizontal dimension.[13]

In one instance, however, the interests of emancipated Jewry and those of mainstream Judaism do converge and dictate the same stance, namely, when the separation of state and church carries its minimal signification— that is, when it merely signifies the disestablishment of religion and not its exclusion from the horizontal dimension. Both parties should favor disestablishment, though the rationale operating in the two cases is quite different and indeed, as we have seen, so is the religion involved. For

---

[12]This opposition to the rise of civil religion manifested in some circles of emancipated Jewry is not to be equated with the opposition dictated by mainstream Judaism. The similarity is only on the surface—both oppose the rise of civil religion. The respective reasons, however, that lead to the stance are diametrically opposed. The emancipated Jew does not want to have any religion, not even a civil religion, in the horizontal dimension.

[13]We should note, however, that the religion referred to in connection with the structure of faith of mainstream Judaism is specifically and exclusively Judaism, while the religion referred to in connection with emancipated Jewry is the religion of the host nation or religion in general. As such, my comparison between the stance taken by emancipated Jewry and the stance dictated by mainstream Jewry is not quite legitimate, since the two stances refer not to the same entity but to different entities. I adjust my analysis below to take care of this discrepancy.

emancipated Jewry it is the religion of the host nation, while for Judaism, it is the religion of Judaism itself. The rationale for the stance taken by emancipated Jewry has already been elucidated above. I attempt here to elucidate the rationale for the stance of mainstream Judaism.

To begin with, one may first note that there is no rationale flowing from the structure of mainstream Judaism that requires the establishment of religion. As I have maintained, the fundamental criterion is that the horizontal dimension be available to religion, that is, to Judaism. But this requirement in no way implies that Judaism must be established. The all-determining criterion thus remains neutral to the question of establishment: it does not dictate support for the establishment of religion, nor does it oppose it. The absence of support for establishment or, conversely, the absence of opposition to disestablishment may be taken as tacit support for disestablishment.

The rationale can be established, I believe, more directly and explicitly. It can be established on the ground that, since the faith of mainstream Judaism is "prophetic" rather than "priestly,"[14] it clearly implies opposition to the establishment of religion. It does so because, in its perspective, the vocation of religion is to become the conscience and critic of society and the state; such a vocation cannot be carried out in the context of establishment. One cannot very well discharge the duties of conscience and critic when one is at the same time supported and maintained by that which is to be criticized. Religion cannot be a function of the state, one of its various departments, and at the same time properly fulfill its task of sitting in judgment over the state. The offices of king and priest may be combined but not the offices of king and prophet. The prophetic type has, therefore, a direct and explicit rationale for opposing the establishment of religion, and inasmuch as the faith of mainstream Judaism does belong to the prophetic type, it likewise is led to oppose the establishment of religion by this same direct and explicit rationale.

The whole analysis thus far necessarily implicates a Judaism that operates, so to speak, in its own backyard, in a situation where its adherents have sovereignty over the horizontal dimension; in short, it implies the placement

---

[14]We obviously cannot go here into a detailed justification of this claim. It may suffice, however, to point rather briefly and somewhat dogmatically to the fact that an essential distinguishing mark of the prophetic type, in contradistinction to the priestly type, is its requirement for religion to be involved in the horizontal dimension. In such a case, the structure of faith of mainstream Judaism clearly belongs to the prophetic type, since it requires, by its very essence, the involvement of religion in the horizontal dimension.

of Judaism in the context of a Jewish state. For the analysis here has been based on the claim that the structure of faith of Judaism requires the horizontal dimension for itself so it can rightfully appropriate and impinge upon it. This situation can be secured only in the context of sovereignty, that is, only in the context of Jewish statehood. Strictly speaking, therefore, the conclusions of the analysis thus far apply only in the case when Judaism is situated in its own "home," when it is the dominant religion of the community that wields sovereignty over the horizontal dimension.[15]

This observation suggests that the conclusions derived from the analysis thus far have no applicability in the context of the diaspora, where Judaism is not situated in its home. The only possible implication for the diaspora situation (and it is an ancillary consideration) is to intimate that it would ill behoove Judaism to criticize other religions (for example, Christianity) for opposing separation of state and church in the context of their own respective homes, seeing that it itself, when situated in the context of

---

[15]Indeed, in the reestablished state of israel, where Judaism is in its home, there is no separation of church and state or civil religion. Furthermore, the right and the propriety of Judaism's involvement in the horizontal dimension is accepted by Jewry almost universally. For there is no denying that the vast majority of Jewry desires and, indeed, considers it essential and right that the state be specifically a Jewish state and not only a state where Jews live. This clearly means, however, that Judaism's impingement on the horizontal dimension must be accepted and validated; for without such impingement the state cannot really be a Jewish state. Thus, when Judaism is the dominant religion, as is in the case in the state of Israel, there is really no opposition to involving religion in the horizontal dimension.

Many Jews are unhappy with the religious situation prevailing in the state of Israel. This problem, I believe, is due specifically to the fact that Judaism here utilizes the power of the state to impose itself on the community, that it is constituted as the established religion. Furthermore, for some (though by no means all), there is the further consideration that has nothing to do with the *status* of Judiasm but that rather impinges on the *kind* of Judaism involved. Namely, I suggest that the unhappiness and opposition is also due, at least in part, to the fact that the Judaism established here is Orthodox Judaism. Indeed, a case can be made that, while Orthodoxy was a most suitable expression for diaspora existence, it is not a suitable expression for existing in a reestablished state and that consequently its imposition in the context of the reestablished state is bound to cause conflict and opposition. In any case, these considerations—i.e., that Judaism is constituted as an established religion and that its expression is Orthodoxy—in no way countermand the claims of our analysis above (if anything, the opposition to establishment actually conforms with the analysis above). What would have presented a serious problem is an opposition to Judaism's impingement upon the horizontal dimension. Such opposition, I submit, has by and large not occurred.

its own home, pursues the same opposition. If Judaism, as we have argued, must demand the right to impinge in its own home upon the horizontal dimension, it must grant to other religions the right to do the same in their respective homes.

Neither the conclusions nor the very form and substance of the analysis pursued thus far are to the point, as far as the context of the diaspora is concerned. For there the analysis has based itself on the criterion that the horizontal dimension must be available to Judaism, and therefore its main question centered on how the separation of state and church would impinge on that availability. But in the context of diaspora this criterion and this question are completely beside the point, since there Judaism has no rightful claim on the horizontal dimension to begin with.

In the context of diaspora, the relevant criterion must be formulated in terms of the viability and survival of Judaism. For in diaspora, Judaism is perforce passive, receiving the action of others. It is, therefore, not so much the question of what Judaism does and requires as the question of what others (that is, the host nations) do and how it affects the prospects for the viability and survival of Judaism. Issues of state-church separation and the rise of civil religion, when enjoined in diaspora, clearly involve not Judaism but the host religion. The host religion and not Judaism is to be separated from the state; its place and function is to be supplanted by the rise of a civil religion. Although these issues do not directly involve Judaism, they certainly may affect Judaism as regards its prospects for viability and survival. To determine, therefore, the stance that diaspora Judaism should take toward these issues, we must examine them with a view as to how they impinge upon the prospects of the viability and survival of Judaism in diaspora.

III

In light of this new criterion that is applicable to the context of diaspora, it is not too difficult to see that the separation of state and church in all its three significations actually holds a certain advantage for Judaism when it is placed in diaspora. For in all three significations the act of separation clearly reduces the power and influence of the host religion. Given the threat that a host religion inescapably presents for Judaism when placed in diaspora, such reduction in the power and influence of the host religion should clearly work to the advantage of Judaism.

Similarly, one can see that the rise of civil religion may well hold a possible advantage for Judaism inasmuch as civil religion is likely to be more neutral and less threatening toward a minority religion than a host religion that is a traditional religion. A civil religion is likely to transcend the factors that lead to mutual rejection, friction, and intolerance between traditional religions, which are due primarily to the doctrinal and historical differences between them. But it is precisely these differences that a civil religion is likely to neutralize or at least reduce—when (as the case often may be) it is a watered-down version of a traditional religion or, said differently, when it is a religion grounded in some pervasive humanitarian-ethnic precepts or in some aspects of universal human reason and experience. A civil religion will certainly not be a religion grounded in doctrinal confessions or symbolic expressions that are determined by revelation or by history, and this factor, after all, is the crux of the matter. To a considerable extent, the rise of civil religion thus cleans the slate, so to speak, and introduces a new context in which, on the surface at least, Judaism is accorded a more equal footing with the traditional religion of the host nation. This arrangement can certainly be viewed as presenting a more congenial and advantageous situation for Judaism.

It would seem, therefore, that both the separation of state and church and the rise of civil religion are advantageous for Judaism when it is placed in diaspora. A closer and more careful examination shows, however, that they are not purely advantageous, that coupled with the advantages they also present possible disadvantages. Indeed, these possible disadvantages are implicated in every one of the various formulations in which the notions of the state-church separation and of civil religion express themselves.

One can argue that the disestablishment of religion presents not only the advantage of reducing the power and influence of the host religion but also the possible disadvantage that, in all likelihood, Judaism too will be deprived of a measure of recognition and support from the state. For it is a curious fact that, by and large, the establishment of the host religion tends to involve the state with the other nonestablished religions in its domain; indeed, when the religious climate is not too intolerant, the tendency is for the state to bestow some measure of formal recognition and support on these nonestablished religions. From a practical vantage point, such recognition and support, though it be minimal and, in a way, given in a left-handed manner, can nonetheless be very beneficial and helpful to a minority religion such as Judaism. In the adverse conditions of diaspora existence, where none or only very few of the necessary external proppings in support of the institution of religion are available, any support or recognition from the state can only be helpful. Such support, however, would be clearly lost in the context of disestablishment.[16]

---

[16]It would be interesting to compare in this connection how Judaism fares, both in the short and in the long run, in such countries as, for example, Great Britain and the United States.

Likewise, one can argue that in the "wall of separation" formulation, where the advantage accrued to Judaism from the elimination of the power and influence of the host religion is most pronounced, a most serious situation for Judaism is also present. One must inquire as to what would come to take place of the host religion in characterizing the horizontal dimension. In all probability, a thoroughgoing secularism or, in a context where a civil religion has arisen, a civil religion that is some form of neopaganism would take the place of the host religion. These alternatives are potentially much more detrimental to the viability and survival of Judaism than the traditional religion of the host nation is likely to be, particularly when the latter (as is likely to be the case) is a sister biblical faith (for example, Christianity). Surely a thoroughgoing secularism is more inimical to Judaism than any religion may be (no matter how hostile toward Judaism it may be), while in the whole spectrum of religions no religious formulation is further removed from Judaism than paganism.[17] Paganism represents the fundamental alternative to biblical faith, and consequently it is, in the last analysis, the real antagonist to Judaism, one that can become most virulent.[18] Thus, commensurate to the pronounced advantage that the "wall of separation" formulation presents to Judaism, the disadvantage that it may also entail is equally serious. Indeed, in the last analysis, the disadvantage may well outweigh the advantage, and Judaism may well be placed here in the position of having jumped from the frying pan into the fire.

Finally, one can argue that even the "line of division" formulation—where, *on balance,* the situation for Judaism is probably most advantageous—may be threatening. For the "line of division" formulation creates a situation that is much more congenial for the assimilation of emancipated Jewry into the environment of its host nation. This greater tolerance exists only be-

---

[17]Secularism and paganism are in fact not all that different. They are really two sides of the same coin in the sense that ultimately both establish blind power as the ultimate principle of the universe. One may perhaps say that paganism is the imaginative-mythical expression, while secularism is the rational-scientific expression, but both ultimately share the same weltanschauung. It should thus not be surprising that secularism and neopaganism go hand in hand here as the two alternative substitutes. A consistent inner logic dictates such a relation.

[18]A good case can be made that the virulent, specifically anti-Judaism strain within Christianity is due to its paganization, namely, that it expresses itself essentially in Hellenistically grounded Christianity rather than in Hebraically grounded Christianity. As such, here too one really encounters, in the last analysis, paganism.

cause the formulation diminishes the presence of the host religion; even more pertinently, the civil religion that it is likely to substitute for the host religion is far less of a barrier to the process of assimilation. A civil religion that is a watered-down, nondescript version of the host religion, that emphasizes universally accepted ethical principles, and that suppresses the particularity of history and doctrine (and especially when it may also extend its base to encompass the heritage of Judaism) is much more inviting and much more likely to be embraced by emancipated Jewry than is the traditional religion of the host nation. Such a civil religion would clearly mitigate many of the intellectual and psychological barriers that the traditional religion presents, with all its doctrinal, ritualistic, and symbolic baggage. As such, the civil religion can only enhance the process of assimilation. Such assimilation may suit the interests and desires of emancipated Jewry, but it is certainly most threatening to the viabilty and survival of Judaism. Judaism is threatened not only by force and persecution but also, sad and ironic as it may be, by acceptance and assimilation. This latter alternative does not inflict the suffering of rejection, nor does it threaten Judaism with physical extermination. Indeed, if anything, it extends the generosity of embrace. Though it be an embrace, however, it is nonetheless the embrace of death, of spiritual extinction.

The "line of division" formulation thus also has its disadvantageous aspect. Indeed, it is a most insidious aspect inasmuch as its threat is not readily apparent. It is delivered, so to speak, concealed, wrapped in a package that is most appealing to the emancipated Jew; or, to change the metaphor, its bitter pill comes coated with the most enticing flavor. Furthermore, in the context of the situation that basically prevails today in the West, it represents the more imminent threat. In an enlightened and tolerant environment, such as basically characterizes the Western democracies today, the threat of assimilation is more serious than the threat of persecution.

We can therefore see again that, in this formulation as in the other two alternative formulations, the stance of diaspora Judaism is equivocal regarding both the separation of state and church and civil religion. One can see advantages but also disadvantages; indeed, the more favorable the advantages, the more serious are the disadvantages.

IV

We have seen that, in attempting to analyze the Jewish position regarding civil religion and church-state separation, one must actually deal with three different entities—with emancipated Jewry, with Judaism taken in terms of its structure of faith (that is, when it is placed in the context of its own home), and with Judaism when it is placed in the context of diaspora. Furthermore, we have also seen that, as regards the implication of religion in the issues before us, one is actually confronted with two basically different situations—one where the religion implicated as Judaism itself and another where the host religion is other than Judaism.

Last, and most significantly, we have seen that the Jewish position regarding the issues before us really comprises three distinct and different stances: (1) an essentially positive stance when dealing with emancipated Jewry, (2) an essentially negative stance when dealing with Judaism in terms of its structure of faith, and (3) an essentially equivocal stance when dealing with Judaism in the context of diaspora. Indeed, given the two former observations, this last observation, which constitutes the very essence of our analysis here, should not be surprising. For clearly the stance of Judaism or, for that matter, of emancipated Jewry would be affected by whether the religion implicated in these issues is Judaism or another religion. Even more pertinently, it is clearly and directly affected by the first observation, namely, by the fact that there are three different entities involved here. With respect to Judaism when viewed in terms of its structure of faith, the determining criterion is the availability of the horizontal dimension. With respect to Judaism when viewed in the context of diaspora, it is the viability and survival of Judaism. And with respect to emancipated Jewry, it is integration (or assimilation) into the horizontal dimension belonging to the host nation. Clearly, these criteria are not compatible; consequently, it is inescapable that three different and, indeed, contradictory stances would emerge here.

One must conclude, therefore, that the Jewish position toward the issues of the separation of state and church and of state and church and of civil religion is far from univocal. Certainly, it is not just the wholeheartedly supportive stance taken by emancipated Jewry. The Jewish position, when taken in all its dimensions, is much more equivocal and, on balance, much less supportive.

Indeed, a good case can be made that, even with respect to emancipated Jewry, its position too ought to be less supportive. For one can argue that the supportive position of emancipated Jewry is due to the fact that its perception of the situation has a blind spot. As we have seen above, the strongly supportive position of emancipated Jewry flows from the fact that it perceives the host religion as the ultimate barrier to full integration. There can be no denying that the host religion indeed serves as a barrier, and consequently the inner logic underlying the position of emancipated Jewry is quite valid as far as it goes. But it does not go far enough. For another factor serves as a barrier to the full integration of emancipated Jewry, namely, the ethnic factor. Indeed, this factor is a more obdurate and pernicious barrier to integration than is the religious factor. The ethnic rather than the religious factor, particularly in the circumstances of the modern world, really stresses and aggravates the exclusion of the Jew. Emancipated Jewry, however, fails to take account of this factor in formulating its position toward the issues before us. It fails to see that, even if the host religion and indeed all religions are totally removed, it would still be excluded from full integration by the ethnic factor. Here lies the blind spot in emancipated Jewry's perception of its situation.[19]

If the ethnic factor is brought into the picture, then the position taken by emancipated Jewry, specifically its wholehearted support for the "wall of separation" formulation and its corresponding civil religion, must be reassessed. For, as we have noted above, one must ask in these circumstances what comes to take the place of the host religion? The answer is a thoroughgoing secularism or a civil religion that is some form of neopaganism. But both secularism and neopaganism are much more likely to stress the ethnic differentiation than when the host religion is a biblical faith. As such, in light of this consideration and our observation regarding the pernicious nature of the ethnic factor, the "wall of separation" formulation should be really viewed as a hindrance rather than as an opening toward the integration of emancipated Jewry. By its very inner logic, determined as it is by the search for full integration, emancipated Jewry should therefore view the "wall of separation" formulation as being more inimical to its interests than the presence of the host religion.

The position of emancipated Jewry when it is based in reality and not in illusion—namely, when it takes into account the ethnic factor—is thus brought somewhat closer to the position of Judaism when placed in the context of the diaspora. At least with regard to the "wall of separation" formulation, the position of emancipated Jewry should now be much closer to the position of Judaism when placed in the context of diaspora. Of course, I do not suggest that the difference between the two positions is removed altogether. Indeed, with regard to the other two formulations, the differ-

---

[19]That the emancipated Jew is inclined to overlook the factor of ethnic differentiation is actually quite understandable. This factor, in contrast to the factor of religious differentiation, is a given that no one can change. It is, indeed, ultimate in the sense that it is inextricable. As such, however, it is understandable that the emancipated Jew, in the desire for full integration, would be inclined to ignore or even deny the reality of this factor. One is inclined to ignore or deny uncomfortable realities. Emancipated Jews believe and act on the supposition that only the religious factor differentiates them from their host nation and that, if the religious factor were to be removed, the road to full integration would be unobstructed.

ence delineated above remains; these formulations are not really affected by considerations of the ethnic factor, and consequently the position of emancipated Jewry with respect to them is not changed. That a difference between the two positions remains should not, however, be surprising. In the last analysis, the fact remains that the criterion determining the position of emancipated Jewry (that is, the criterion of full integration into the horizontal dimension of the host nation) and the criterion determining the position of Judaism when placed in the context of diaspora (that is, the criterion of the viability and survival of Judaism) are in conflict. Integration into a horizontal dimension that is not Jewish necessarily signifies a weakening of the viability and a threat to the survival of Judaism. In a nutshell, this tension is the fundamental problematic that the emancipation precipitates for Judaism.

THE CROWDED PUBLIC SQUARE: A CRITIQUE OF RICHARD JOHN NEUHAUS ON CIVIL RELIGION

Ralph C. Wood

Liberals and conservatives alike seem agreed that we Americans are a religious people. The Declaration of Independence, the Great Seal, the Pledge of Allegiance, and the National Anthem all contain overt references to the God who has favored our undertaking and who thus is our trust. The idea that the United States is a nation uniquely favored of God has been voiced by every president from Episcopalian Washington to Presbyterian Wilson, from Baptist Truman to Catholic Kennedy. Yet the vexing question remains: what are the political consequences of our inveterate religiousness?

Many on the religious right call for Christianity to be made the official religion of the nation. Only then, in their view, can this people become what John Winthrop and Abraham Lincoln envisioned: "a city upon a hill" and "the last best hope of earth." The religious left, solicitous for the rights of non-Christians and even of nonbelievers, prefers to speak of religious values that are common to everyone. If God is to be invoked at all, it is as theologically unspecific Supreme Being. In this chapter I argue the proposition that these two viewpoints are not as opposed as they may seem, that in fact they are mirror versions of each other, and that we thus need a new model for the relation of civil and confessional faith—a model I shall define as "the crowded public square."

THE NAKED PUBLIC SQUARE

The figure of Richard John Neuhaus provides an ideal case in point for my argument. He gives brilliant personal expression to the opposition that is in fact a likeness—the opposition between a nontheological civil religion and the idea of a Christian America. Neuhaus constitutes, in fact, a bristling paradox: he is a Lutheran whose favorite word is "law" rather than "gospel," a closet Tillichian and overt Niebuhrian with deep sympathies for Jerry Falwell and the Moral Majority, and thus a Christian who speaks more often about democracy than about the kingdom of God.

Recently appointed as religion editor for William Buckley's *National Review,* Neuhaus is a liberal who got "mugged by reality," as the neoconservatives like to say. Together with Michael Novak, he helped establish the Institute for Religion and Democracy—an organization that summons Christians and Jews to the political task of providing a self-critical legitimation of American democracy. "In helping to sustain the democratic experiment," reads Neuhaus's originating credo for the institute, "the churches act not only in their own interest but in the interests of humankind."[1]

Already in his 1975 book *Time toward Home: The American Experiment as Revelation,* Neuhaus was sounding what was to become his trumpeted call:

> The most promising gamble is the interplay between explicit biblical religion and the American tradition of public piety. . . . They exist in a symbiotic relationship, each supporting and, to some extent, checking the other. . . . As a false religion Americanism must be repudiated; as the piety of a people "under God," Americanism must be purified and revitalized. . . . Democracy should be inculcated with religious seriousness for the Kingdom's sake.[2]

With the 1984 publication of *The Naked Public Square: Religion and Democracy in America,* Neuhaus has given his thesis full and impressive argument. It is focused upon three clear and closely related theses: (1) that we Americans are an incorrigibly religious people whose national life is premised upon belief in God; (2) that, by an outrageous denial of our fundamental identity, this public piety has been ousted from the marketplace of ideas and values; and thus (3) that the chief political duty of the contem-

---

[1]*Christianity and Democracy: A Statement of the Institute on Religion and Democracy,* 9.

[2]Richard J. Neuhaus, *Time Toward Home: The American Experiment as Revelation* (New York: Seabury, 1975) 19, 190, 204.

porary church is to reforge the ancient link between democratic freedom and Judeo-Christian faith.

America as a Religious, Even a Christian Nation

Neuhaus is not at all squeamish about using the phrases "a Christian people" and "a Christian nation." He does so despite the warning from a Jewish friend, "When I hear the term 'Christian America,' I see barbed wire."[3] Neuhaus claims to employ the locution in a purely descriptive and sociological sense, not as a normative theological and political ideal. Yet he can scarcely conceal his glee over the results of a survey of North Carolinians taken in the 1970s. It revealed that they overwhelmingly affirm the following propositions: "Human rights come from God and not merely from laws," the United States flag is "sacred," and "America is God's chosen nation today" (81). Unlike Walker Percy's Binx Bolling, who will not search after a God whom 98 percent of the American populace has already found, Neuhaus is cheered by the statistical evidence against our much-touted pluralism: "Over ninety percent of the American people say they believe in God and think the Judeo-Christian tradition is somehow normative for personal and public life" (145).

This ingrained American religiosity is not the momentary product of the Great Awakening, of nineteenth-century revivals, or of the contemporary Evangelical insurgency. It is something intrinsic, Neuhaus argues, even to the supposedly deistic faith of the Founding Fathers. Madison, Jefferson, Washington, Franklin, and the Adamses were all agreed that, while the state could not favor any one of the Christian sects, it was not at all hostile to their independent well-being. On the contrary, the Founders were so confident that the various churches would provide moral reinforcement for republican virtue that they rejected Rousseau's call for a civil religion to motivate and sanction our public ethic.

Neuhaus makes a convincing case that, unlike most other nations, the United States was a people before it was a polity. We are a nation by intent and purpose, a union fabricated out of ideas and beliefs rather than blood and soil. This created thing named America presupposes what Neuhaus calls "a culture of virtue" (141) sustained by religion. John Adams declared, in a celebrated statement, that "we have no government armed with power capable of contending with human passions unbridled by morality and religion. Our constitution was made only for a moral and religious people.

---

[3]Richard J. Neuhaus, *The Naked Public Square: Religion and Democracy in America* (Grand Rapids MI: Eerdmans, 1984) 145. All further references to this work will be made within parentheses.

It is wholly inadequate for the government of any other'' (95). In his Farewell Address, President Washington cautioned against the notion that "morality can be maintained without religion." And James Madison insisted that "he who would be a citizen in civil society must first be considered a subject of the divine governor of nature."

Even the scoffing Jefferson, who regarded Christian orthodoxy as monkish superstition, asked—in his condemnation of slavery —whether "the liberties of a nation [can] be thought secure when we have removed their only firm basis, a conviction in the minds of the people that these liberties are the gift of God? That they are not to be violated but with his wrath? Indeed I tremble for my country," concluded Jefferson, "when I reflect that God is just; that his justice cannot sleep forever; that . . . the Almighty has no attribute which can take side with us [on slavery]" (100). The deep theological ruminations of Lincoln's Second Inaugural could also be cited as evidence for the inexorably religious character of the American nation and people. So can the rulings of Supreme Court Justice Douglas, even though he sought first the welfare of the environment rather the kingdom of God: "We are a religious people," said he, "whose institutions presuppose a Supreme Being" (80).

The Exile of Religion from the Public Square

Neuhaus agrees with the "popular intuition" (81) that our inexpungable religiousness ought to make a difference in matters that matter. It vexes him deeply that our national piety has been exiled from the public square. He refers not merely to the banning of manger scenes from courthouse lawns but to important legal cases where religious arguments about abortion, sanity, or any other morally debatable subject are ruled literally out of court. Neuhaus cites the notorious *Abington* case of 1963, where the Supreme Court outlawed the practice of Bible reading in government schools. For the first time, says Neuhaus, an invidious distinction was drawn between religious freedom and religious observance. While the government must guarantee the former, this new ruling forbids the state to make any provision for the latter. What had previously been a government guarantee of freedom *for* religion, argues Neuhaus, has now become a government insistence on freedom *from* religion (101).

Neuhaus's thesis is that the United States, until very recently, has had a quasi-religious government vitally dependent upon the moral legitimation of a nonestablished church. We have not had a double tradition of religious freedom and religious practice, Neuhaus insists, but a single tradition that shares—as he quotes Glen Thurow—"a common root in recognition of presumed spiritual needs and institutional dependency on a Supreme Being" (101). Recent court rulings and government edicts have given us, instead, a pseudosecular state that is officially neutral toward religion. There is but a short leap, Neuhaus warns, from neutrality to hostility. And once the state ousts religion from the public arena, it has no countervailing force to check its pretensions. Whether its politics be leftist or rightist, the religiously neutral state seeks to become omnicompetent and all providing; in a word, totalitarian.

Far from having been intended to ensure the government's religious neutrality, the nonestablishment clause was meant for the protection of the church rather than the state. Only as the nation is accountable to what Neuhaus calls a transcendent purpose and critique can it be guarded against the allurement of absoluteness. The First Amendment was written precisely to ensure this transcendent judgment and legitimation of government—not, says Neuhaus, "to prevent the church from taking over the state but to prevent the state from taking over the church" (116). Yet the church's task of religiously supporting and limiting the state cannot be performed, Neuhaus contends, when religion itself is relegated to the merely private sphere of opinion and preference. When fundamentalists inveigh against the evils of secular humanism, says Neuhaus, they fail to recognize that the true threat lies in this sinister privatizing of religion.

By its very nature, Neuhaus maintains, Judeo-Christian religion is a public affair. Jews and Christians are committed to the anti-Platonic proposition that the purposes of God are made manifest within the particularities of history. Biblical faith, Neuhaus insists, is not centered upon individualistic longing for otherworldly salvation. Though Jews and Christians both look forward to the coming messianic age, they share a fundamental urgency about the well-being of this present world. Such religious devotion to the commonwealth requires, in turn, the generation and inculcation of transcendent moral values that provide what Peter Berger calls "a sacred canopy" for culture. Because the American democratic state is fundamentally a religious and not a secular enterprise, the church must remain the chief bearer of moral legitimation for our culture. Unless we act, therefore, to restore religion to the public square, we will have suffered what Neuhaus defines as an unconscionable fate: "the outlawing of the basis of law" (259).

The Summons to Rejoin Religion and Democracy

Both the liberal and the conservative defection from this central Judeo-Christian task arouses Neuhaus's ire. He is not critical of fundamentalists, therefore, for asserting the public meaning of the gospel. On the contrary, he argues that Martin King and Jerry Falwell—however much they may differ on other matters —are agreed in their determination to "disrupt the business of secular America by an appeal to religiously based values" (78).

Contemporary fundamentalists are simply practicing the lessons that old-line liberals have so clearly taught them.

Neuhaus criticizes fundamentalism for the failure to base its religious appeal upon principles that are accessible to the general public. In refusing to enter moral discourse with those who lie outside the circle of true believers, fundamentalists condemn themselves to the same privatized and apolitical religion they seek to escape:

> A dilemma, both political and theological, facing the religious new right is simply this: *it wants to enter the political arena making public claims on the basis of private truths.* The integrity of politics itself requires that such a proposal be resisted. Public decisions must be made by arguments that are public in character. A public argument is transsubjective. It is not derived from sources of revelation or disposition that are essentially private and arbitrary. The perplexity of fundamentalism in public is that its self-understanding is premised upon a view of religion that is emphatically not public in character. (36)

Yet it is not chiefly religious conservatives whom Neuhaus seeks to impale upon the point of his Judeo-Christian spear. His real spleen is reserved for religious liberals, who ought to know better than to vacate the public square. It was liberal American religion, after all, that first nourished the dream of democracy as the appropriate political expression of Christian faith. "The main line of the mainline story," writes Neuhaus, "was confidence and hope regarding the Americanizing of Christianity and the Christianizing of America" (219). From Horace Bushnell to Washington Gladden to Lyman Abbott, the great religious liberals of the nineteenth-century were all pledged to the claim that America is a redeemer nation destined to fulfill humanity's future. "If we want the nations to understand Christianity," wrote Gladden, "we have got to have a Christianized nation to show them" (209). Neuhaus quotes Robert Handy's summation of this nineteenth-century call for a Christian America: "The nation itself as bearer of civilization was elevated as an agency of the subjugation of the world to Christ" (211).

Neuhaus chastizes liberals of the last century not for the wrongness of their central premise but for failing to heed the warnings of their best critics—Hawthorne and Melville, Whitman and Emerson. These secular sages prophesied against the cultural smugness and optimistic self-assurance of the nation's unofficial Protestant establishment, even as others were later to criticize its neglect of the miraculous and transcendent in Christianity. The Social Gospel movement, which should have constituted the Third Great Awakening in American religion and culture, instead became what Neuhaus calls the Great Accommodation and what Handy labels the Second Disestablishment. Once Roosevelt's New Deal had legislated the very economic reforms that the Christianizers of the economic order had clamored for, there was not much left for Social Gospelers to do—except, as Neuhaus wickedly suggests, to pray for "the second coming of George McGovern, assuming that FDR is no longer available" (231).

Neuhaus believes that liberation theology—as the late twentieth-century heir of the Social Gospel movement—has repeated the same mistake as its predecessor, though inverting it in the process. Whereas old-style liberals made a naively uncritical endorsement of American culture, new liberationists make a naively judgmental denunciation of it. These new secularizers of the gospel have put themselves out of all business except the business of complaint. "If those in control of the dominant forces of our time do not want our help," Neuhaus satirizes disaffected mainliners, "then we will seek out the opposition to those forces and find our meaning in helping them to overthrow their oppressors" (225).

Neuhaus makes caustic commentary on the fluffy romanticism inherent in the liberationist call for a return to the servant church, to "the church of the catacombs, the persecuted church, the adversarial church, the church of the poor" (226). It may be much harder to be a Christian when the church is ignored, Neuhaus observes, than when it is attacked. To make persecution and opposition the defining marks of true faith is no less a secularizing of the church, Neuhaus argues, than to make a triumphalist identification of Christianity and American culture.

> The trinity of Christianity—America—civilization may have been naive and discredited, but probably no more so than the current bureaucratized [i.e., World Council of Churches] obeisance to the trinity of Christianity—third world —revolutionary justice. . . . At least the first version engaged American Christians "where they live" and resulted in more than memos for a revolution, the noise of prophetic assemblies, and pervasive feelings of failure and guilt. (237)

There is considerable merit, Neuhaus believes, in the much-maligned civil religion called Christendom. Without its cultural transmission of Christian faith, Neuhaus acerbically notes, most of us would not be Christians at all. Thus does he call the contemporary church to the culture-forming task of giving self-critical support to the American experiment in democratic freedom. In words redolent of Reinhold Niebuhr's work, Neuhaus confidently declares that "Christians may see in democracy a development under divine guidance. Democracy is the appropriate form of governance in a fallen creation in which no person or institution can infallibly speak for God. Democracy is the necessary expression of humility in which all persons and institutions are held accountable to the transcendent purpose imperfectly discerned." (116)

THE CROWDED PUBLIC SQUARE

Neuhaus's argument would not be worthy of criticism were it not so nearly persuasive. He has established the substantial connection between

American religion and American democracy. He has shown how religious values have been driven out of the public square. And he has challenged conservatives and liberals alike to embrace the culture-chaping conse-quences of Christian faith. Yet, for all that is right in his analysis, Neuhaus has erred in three important ways that must be addressed: (1) historically, he has collapsed civil and confessional faith into a falsely undifferentiated unity; (2) theologically, he has ignored the deep tensions between even the highest humanist wisdom and the self-revelation of God in Israel and Christ; and (3) ecclesiologically, he has failed to discern how particularized com-munities of faith—and not a generalized American Christianity—form the best antidote to the totalitarian temptation. Against Neuhaus's vision of a "theonomous public square" as a replacement for the barren marketplace of values, I shall argue for a crowded public square —where a variety of secular and theological claims are free both to complete and to coincide as the occasion demands.

Civil Piety
versus Confessional Faith at the Founding

Sidney Mead maintains that the American religious tradition of the eigh-teenth-century is not single, as Neuhaus would have it, but double. There was no unitary "American religion" shared by the deistic Framers and their sec-tarian counterparts. There were instead, says Mead, two conflicting tradi-tions: the rationalists and the pietists. Franklin and Jefferson were typical examples of the rationalist party. They had in common their aristocratic standing, their considerable wealth, their paternalistic social sense, and their devotion to learning as the fundamental solution to human problems. Jeffer-son and Franklin respected the pietistic religion of the masses largely because of its social function: it served as a moral brake on the unruly human passions. "Think how great a portion of mankind," wrote Franklin, in marvelous self-exemption, "have need of the motives of religion to restrain them from vice, to support virtue, and retain them in the practice of it till it becomes *habitual,* which is the great point for its security."[4]

Regarding the central theological claims of Christian orthodoxy, Jef-ferson and Franklin were skeptics at best, scoffers at worst. When ques-tioned about the divinity of Jesus, Franklin replied—with supreme condescension—that he saw no harm in believing the doctrine, but he doubted that "the Supreme takes it amiss, by distinguishing the Unbeliev-ers in his Government of the World with any peculiar Mark of his Dis-

---

[4]Quoted in Sidney Mead, *The Lively Experiment: The Shaping of Christianity in America* (New York: Harper & Row, 1976) 44.

pleasure.''[5] Franklin's ''Articles of Belief and Acts of Religion'' are theologically vacuous. There is no mention whatever of the Cross or the Resurrection, of salvation or the forgiveness of sin. To his twelve-point program of self-improvement, Franklin added "humility" almost as an afterthought. The autonomous method of achieving this virtue is even more revealing: "Imitate Jesus and Socrates," says Franklin.[6]

It is not necessary to challenge the Founders' orthodoxy, for Neuhaus never claims that the Framers were men of profound Christian faith. What I am contesting is his failure to differentiate the deistic religion of the Founders from the confessional faith of the Christian sects. As Mead points out, there was a trade-off between the rationalists and the pietists. Framers and revivalists alike feared the persecutorial powers of a nationally established church. Denominationalism and disestablishment thus offered a happy solution for both parties.[7] Yet, by ignoring the Christological barrenness of the Framers' faith, Neuhaus also ignores their merely instrumentalist view of religion as promoting the civic virtue that govenment itself cannot engender.

It was the Founders' conviction that, while doctrines divide, ethics unite. Eternal rewards and punishments are no fit basis, therefore, for civil definitions of right and wrong. Insofar as sectarian Christians remained committed to the suprarational claims of revelation, their religion was a distraction from the primary business of nation building. Neuhaus is correct to notice that the Founders rejected Rousseau's call for a state-sponsored civil religion. Yet George Armstrong Kelly has shown that these same Fathers of the nation also "reached the conclusion that the virtue inspired by religious belief was not adequate to guarantee the stability of a federal republic; a new 'political science,' based on man's more ordinary and profound tendencies, was also necessary."[8] The eighteenth-century religious square was thus a good deal more crowded than Neuhaus acknowledges. The faith of our fathers was not an undifferentiated thing called American religion but a double tradition of deistic civil piety and sectarian confessional faith. Our dual religious tradition also has conflicting political consequences, as I shall seek to demonstrate.

---

[5]Ibid., 45.

[6]Benjamin Franklin, *Autobiography and Other Writings,* ed. Russel B. Nye (Cambridge MA: Houghton Mifflin, 1958) 77.

[7]Mead, *Lively Experiment,* 35-36, 42.

[8]George Armstrong Kelly, *Politics and Religious Consciousness in America* (New Brunswick NJ: Transaction, 1984) 216.

Humanist Wisdom and Divine Revelation

Neuhaus's collapse of necessary historical distinctions is also at work in his own theology. Though he claims an overt debt to Wolfhart Pannenberg, Neuhaus has an unconfessedly Tillichian understanding of religion: "At the heart of culture is religion," Neuhaus writes; "all the ways we think and act and interact [derive from] what we believe is ultimately true and important" (27). Neuhaus knows, of course, that there is danger lurking in this cultural definition of religion as "the obligation that we affirm most deeply, most daringly, and perhaps most desperately" (250). The problem is not merely that the faith of any death-dealing superpatriot or terrorist could be so described. His definition of religion falls prey, more seriously, to the charge of projectionism made by the great masters of suspicion (as Paul Ricoeur calls them): Feuerbach and Marx, Nietzsche and Freud. To guard against the canard that religion is but the sacred canopy that we ourselves erect over our fondest ideals, Neuhaus insists upon the givenness of our deepest and truest commitments:

> Critical to any life worth living is the ordering of our loyalties—accepting responsibility for deciding by what we will be bound. The life without obligations that are freely accepted and faithfully observed is a life in bondage to chaos, a life without meaning. Freedom is found in obedience to the normative; all other liberations are just different ways of being lost. With greater and lesser degrees of reflection, we thus bind ourselves in friendship, in marriage, in vocation, and a host of other decisions. . . . Having decided upon the ordering of our loyalties, [we find that] our loyalties order us. After choosing our obligations, we discover they have chosen us. . . . In theological argot it is like prevenient grace, the grace that is always a step ahead of us, turning our achievements into gifts, our discoveries into revelations, and our choices into the knowledge of being chosen. (250)

This eloquently Augustinian statement reveals what is both best and worst in Neuhaus's theology. That he is articulating a profound piece of humanist wisdom, there is no doubting. He is utterly right to say that we do not create law so much as it creates us. But the givenness of the moral order as something that we do not selfishly invent for the protection of our own power and privilege is not the same thing as the prevenient grace of God. Christians ought to be grateful that the world has an intrinsically ethical shape. We ought also to support and sustain such moral order in its democratic expression. Yet we ought not to confuse humanist wisdom with divine revelation.

Neuhaus fuzzes the theological focus, I believe, when he conflates the two realms into one—as he does in speaking oxymoronically of Judeo-Christian religion, of Christian America, and of Christian humanism. I have yet to meet a Judeo-Christian. There are, in my acquaintance, only Christians and Jews—sons and daughters of a single covenant, I gladly affirm, but in radically different manifestations. "Judeo-Christian" is a term that understandably offends many Jews, because it rests on an Enlightenment reduction of normative Judaism to its supposedly universalistic anticipation of Christianity. The idea of a Christian America ought to be no less odious to Christians. There is but a single Christian people and nation:the body of Christ called the church. Even if our badly divided states were unanimously united in Christian belief, so that every citizen were also a practicing Christian, America would still not be a Christian nation. As modern Israel so vividly demonstrates, ours would be one state among others, not the kingdom of God in the making.

Neuhaus would do well to heed the warning of Karl Barth that all religion—including Christian religion, of course—is a form of unbelief. Religion is often, perhaps even always, the human attempt to live without trust in God. Better still is Barth's caveat about Christian humanism: the noun always controls the adjective—Barth like a good schoolmaster reminds us— and not the other way around. There may indeed be humanist Christians, I would add, but the only good humanist is a secular humanist. It was not Jesus, after all, but Cicero who said, "Omnes homines natura aequales sunt." All men are equal by nature, in the humanist vision, because they are all citizens of single world-society, the cosmopolis. All people are equal in the sight of God, Christians claim, because sin knows no bounds, and yet grace has abounded even more.

Neuhaus grows exceedingly vaporous when he speaks of his own Christian humanism. "Theonomous culture," he tells us vaguely, is one "in which religious and cultural aspirations toward the transcendent are given public expression" (188). "Both Aristotle and Paul," Neuhaus assures us, "when addressing ultimacies, are religious" (140). Neuhaus's preference for the apostle over the "Master Sage of those who know" (as Dante called Aristotle) seems more demographic than theological. Because the vast preponderance of Americans derive their ultimacies from Jerusalem rather than Athens, Neuhaus is not hesitant to speak of the United States as a Christian nation. It is elitist and falsely aristocratic, Neuhaus complains, to demand that our public ethic be derived from classical philosophy rather than biblical religion.

Neuhaus envisions humanist wisdom and Christian revelation as forming a magnificent unity. They are both agreed, he rightly discerns, that life is communal and social before it is private and individual. Yet he ignores the fact that the sociality that they cultivate is enormously different—the one creating a community of freedom and justice for the sake of humanity, the other establishing a society of worship and service for the glory of God. The humanist city is based upon the inherent dignity and rights of human beings; the Christian city is centered upon the shame of the Cross and the surprise of the Resurrection. Neuhaus does indeed speak of a tension between the two cities, but not because their goals are frequently different. It is only because religion has been vacated from the public square, allowing the state to usurp control over the whole of life, that religion must now do battle with politics.

> Thus religion and politics contend for dominance over the same territory. Both are political in the sense of being engaged in a struggle for power. Both are religious in the sense of making a total claim upon life. (Some theological abstractions to the contrary, Christianity *as religion* is engaged in the struggle for power, despite its message being centered upon the powerlessness of the cross.) (131)

"My kingdom is not of this world" is no theological abstraction. This very specific eschatological and political claim will often give offense to humanist wisdom and thus to worldly politics. Neuhaus fails to explain, most noticeably, how civic virtue can be derived from the biblical story of salvation through the always unbidden and often unjust grace of God. Little does he seem to understand what Arthur McGill demonstrated a generation ago: that sin and faith are rarely if ever a set of ethical choices between evil and good. Our basic life-decision lies, according to McGill, between two kinds of power that we must acknowledge as having sway over us and that we must worship as the final Reality of the universe: the power of domination or the power of dispossession. We live and we die, says McGill, "according to the king who holds [us] and the kingdom to which [we] belong."[9]

The great New Testament adjurations are not for Christians to do good, therefore, but to worship and obey the self-surrendering God revealed in Jesus Christ. That such faith and ethics issue also in profound works of human goodness, there is no doubt. Nor is there any gainsaying the deep Christian regard for democratic freedom. The gospel of uncoerced trust in God finds a sure political echo in the idea of government by the consent of the governed. Biblical faith also shares with democratic republicanism the conviction that our species has a deadly propensity for self-aggrandizement, and thus that political restraints must be placed on the governors no less than the governed. Yet, despite these deep affinities between the best human political wisdom and the incomparable salvation revealed in the Jews and the Messiah, there remains a deep gulf separating the two realms. The kingdom of God is not the substance of American culture, and humanist

---

[9]Arthur McGill, *Suffering: A Test Case of Theological Method* (Philadelphia: Westminster, 1982) 92.

democracy is not the shape of Christian faith: they are alternatives sometimes overlapping but often radically opposed.

The Particularized Church
as Antidote to Absolutism

The church as the unique proclaimer and embodiment of this radical gospel is what, in my view, Neuhaus least understands. He declares, in good liberal fashion, that "particularist religious beliefs must somehow be 'translated' into more general terms in order to be admitted into the public arena" (107). This position gets the matter exactly backward. The church makes a decisive witness to culture precisely as it does *not* departicularize its basic story and categories. As George Lindbeck has convincingly shown, the task of the church is not to translate biblical specificities into religious generalities but to convert a vapid people into the concrete and redemptive life-world of God's kingdom. Not translation, therefore, but participation is the central biblical summons. The scriptural stories *shape* the Christian's and the Jew's public identity, argues Linebeck, far more than they *express* a supposedly private encounter with the Numinous that all religions have in common: "To become a Christian involves learning the story of Israel and Jesus well enough to interpret and experience one's self and world in its terms."[10]

Neuhaus's failure to understand the scandalous particularly of biblical faith also leads him to misconstrue the consequences of pluralism. "Pluralism is a jealous god," he complains. "When pluralism is established as dogma, there is no room for other dogmas. The assertion of other points of reference in moral discourse becomes, by definition, a violation of pluralism" (148). Neuhaus is right, as is Secretary of Education William Bennett, to protest against the blandness and sterility of textbooks that are designed to offend no one but that ought to offend everyone: biologies that do not mention evolution, histories that declare Thanksgiving to have been only a harvest festival, psychologies that describe Jesus and Marx as having had obsessive personalities. But Neuhaus is wrong, in my opinion, to put the blame for our cultural calamity on pluralism, chastizing "the minority that claims not to believe the [biblical] story, and the still smaller minority that abhors its being told" (176).

If only Christians were honored by such clear and vigorous opposition! The problem is not secular usurpation so much as it is theological abdication. And surely the church itself is the chief malefactor. No longer really

---

[10]George Lindbeck, *The Nature of Doctrine: Religion and Theology in a Post-liberal Age* (Philadelphia: Fortress, 1984) 34.

believing its own story to be uniquely decisive for the world's salvation, the church has remanded the task of catechesis to the public schools. Left-leaning churches are often little more than counseling centers and social-service agencies operating in the name of happiness and equality. Conservative Christians are busy, for their part, with their own civil religion. Creationism, inerrancy, and the profit motive constitute their very Americanized trinity. Whoring after the same bastard god of relevance, the left-wing and right-wing churches are equally remiss in their failure to become the body of Christ.

If the church rightly assumed its cultural responsibility, it would insist that humanists be humanists and not surrogate saviors. Christians ought, in fact, to be deeply alarmed about the decay of humanism in our time. The problem with our so-called secular humanism is that it is not secular enough. It is a pseudoreligious affair of "caring and sharing" that a Cicero or a Cato, a Jefferson or a Franklin, would find repulsive. Whereas classical humanists knew the tragic limits of their enterprise, many contemporary humanists believe that there is nothing intrinsically crooked and wretched about the human condition. Hence their eagerness to serve up a secular version of salvation. One of the church's chief cultural tasks, therefore, is to hold humanists accountable to the tragic wisdom inherent in their own worldly faith.

Neuhaus is justified in his fear that our idiot humanism and our idiot fundamentalism could issue in an ever so clever totalitarianism. A democratically self-limited state undergirded by a transcendent stress on the right of dissent is, he believes, the best prophylactic against a statist absolutism of either the left or the right. "The religious [and political] freedom of those outside the Judeo-Christian consensus," he writes, "is best protected by grounding such freedom in that consensus" (146). Such serene confidence in a suprachurchly civil religion consisting of conflated Judaism and Christianity is, in my judgment, Neuhaus's most serious error. To rely on the so-called Judeo-Christian-humanist consensus as a guarantee that the Holocaust and Gulag will *never* happen again is, as Stanley Hauerwas has so astutely observed, to create the very conditions under which they are *likely* to happen again.[11]

Hauerwas argues cogently that a religious minority such as the Jews is the first group to be persecuted in the name of our common humanity and a universally valid ethic. It is precisely their stubborn historical uniqueness

---

[11]Stanley Hauerwas, *Against the Nations: War and Survival in a Liberal Society* (Minneapolis: Winston, 1985) 71.

as the particular people of God that make Jews aliens to any consensus politics or religion. Anyone who does not conform to "the common brotherhood of humanity" soon becomes "the enemy of the people." Barbed wire and extermination camps follow. The church and synagogue must never forget, says Hauerwas, the utter scandal of the claim that our lives are controlled by the God of Israel and Christ—not by humanity. Such biblical faith constitutes a profound offense against the Enlightenment assumption that we are a free and self-determining people whenever we emancipate ourselves from all historical particularity. The call of the church, Hauerwas concludes, is not to subsume the Jews within a spurious Constantinian consensus but to make them our covenant partners as God's historically particular and eschatologically expectant people.[12]

My own proposal is not, therefore, to reclothe the naked public square in the bunting of a nonconfessional civil religion called Judeo-Christianity. I plead, instead, for a crowded public square. Let genuine pluralism thrive—not on the naive laissez-faire supposition that countervailing interest groups will, when allowed freely to contend, somehow promote the commonweal, but on the conviction that a profound humanism will keep the church from becoming a dispenser of sociological and psychological aid, even as a vigorous church will keep the state from becoming a surrogate religion. There is no more powerful political force than the church at worship of the Savior slaughtered for our sins and risen for our redemption. If the church were faithful to its historically particular calling as servant of this Messiah who is both coming and come, it would not need to clamor for admission to the political marketplace. It would create a redemptive public space to which the world would come begging for entrance.[13]

---

[12]Ibid., 77.

[13]I am deeply indebted to friends who read and criticized initial drafts of this essay: David Green, Stanley Hauerwas, Robert Utley, and Richard Vance. It also received a helpfully critical reception at the Wake Forest University Philosophy Forum. I want also to thank the Southeastern Association of Baptist Professors of Religion for the kind response given to this essay when it was delivered as the 1987 Presidental Address.

TRANSCENDENT EXPERIENCE AND PSYCHOLOGICAL MODELS OF THE BRAIN

John E. Collins

This chapter considers the meaning of transcendent consciousness from the perspectives of three different psychological theories. These three theories, or models, of the mind/brain represent three different schools of thought in contemporary American psychology and three different positions regarding the solution to one of the most perplexing philosophical problems in Western thought—the problem of the nature of, and relationship between, spirit and matter, or mind and brain.

Arnold Mandell's approach and conclusions are most compatible with the philosophy of materialism or materialistic reductionism. The proponents of this school maintain that matter (brain) is the only reality. For them, spirit (mind) is a secondary reality that results from the complex interactions of material structures and forces. According to this school, when our knowledge is complete, all psychology will be understood by biology, all biology by chemistry, and all chemistry by physics. Charles Tart's psychological theories are, according to my understanding, most compatible with the school of philosophical realism. The proponents of this school maintain that spirit (mind) and matter (brain) are equally real and function interdependently or in complementary ways. Finally, the model of the mind/brain proposed by Karl Pribram can be interpreted in such a way as to be compatible with the school of philosophical idealism, which claims that mind or spirit is the ultimate reality.

A VIEW FROM BELOW:
MANDELL'S NEUROCHEMICAL INTERPRETATION
OF TRANSCENDENT EXPERIENCE

Arnold Mandell is chairman of the Department of Psychiatry in the School of Medicine at the University of California at San Diego. In a lengthy article entitled "Toward a Psychobiology of Transcendence: God in the Brain," he offers a view of the mind-brain problem based on his review of fifteen years of relevant research in neurophysiology and neuropharmacology.[1] He concludes that a "transcendent experience" is a state of consciousness resulting from the loss of serotonin inhibition in the CA_3 type of pyramidal cells of the hippocampus.

The Normal Function of the Hippocampus

In order to understand how an unusual chemical change in the hippocampus leads to the experience of transcendence, it is necessary first to understand, in a general and admittedly simplistic way, how the hippocampus normally functions. The hippocampus is a small organ in the midbrain, or mammalian brain, or Lymbic system. One of its functions is to integrate two highly complex neurocircuits. One circuit, or information flow, that enters the hippocampus is what I shall call the external circuit. This circuit presents information about external objects—information that comes not only directly from the senses but also from the parts of the brain that store descriptions and understandings of external objects. For example, as I look at the apple on my desk, the hippocampus receives the information from optical circuitry that something interesting is present. Almost simultaneously it receives the information from optical circuitry that identifies this particular object as an apple. The cortex also supplies any additional data that seems relevant. For example, it may further inform the hippocampus that the apple is a Winesap or a Golden Delicious, or that it has been on the desk for a week and it may be overripe, or that the apple was placed there by a student, and so forth. In this way the external circuit provides information about objects. Some of this information comes from the brain's memory banks. Even so, this information may be called objective because

---

[1] Arnold Mandell, "Toward a Psychobiology of Transcendence: God in the Brain," in J. Davidson and R. Davidson, eds., *The Psychobiology of Human Consciousness* (New York: Plenum Press, 1980). Hereafter in this section, page citations in the text refer to Mandell's article.

it is perceived to have been derived from previous contact with either the object in question or with other objects so similar as to give information applicable to the present object.

In addition to, and simultaneous with, the information from the external circuit, the hippocampus also receives input from various parts of the body, including parts of the brain that store information about the self. This second circuit, which I call the internal circuit, presents all the relevant subjective information to the hippocampus. For example, information may come from the digestive system that says, "I'm empty," or there may be presented a feeling of guilt in not having eaten the apple and letting it go to waste, or a feeling of appreciation for the student who left the apple, and so on. One of the primary functions of the hippocampus is to integrate these two circuits (that is, to evaluate the information offered by these circuits) and, if it seems appropriate, to initiate the necessary response of the organism to this complex of information. For example, the hippocampus may initiate a sequence of neuroevents that results in eating the apple or throwing it in the wastebasket, or it may initiate a sequence of neuroevents that will result in the attention being turned from the apple and back to writing this chapter.

The Abnormal Hippocampus
and Transcendent Consciousness

Under normal circumstances the hippocampus functions rather smoothly as mediator between the external world and the internal world. Information is received, integrated, and evaluated, and appropriate responses are initiated. But psychologists have been aware for some time that, under certain unusual conditions, the natural safety mechanisms of the brain may lead to a radical departure from this normal process. The following story about some of Pavlov's dogs illustrates this phenomenon (401). In order to study the nature of anxiety and hyperactivity, Pavlov and his colleagues used behavioral techniques to induce states of severe anxiety in several dogs. Some of these dogs were inadvertently left helpless in a tank that was being filled with water. When this was discovered, some were at the point of death. After they were rescued, however, it was found quite unexpectedly that the conditioning of the dogs had been fully obliterated. As a matter of fact, the previously highly anxious and hyperactive dogs were now quite calm and peaceful. They seemed to have obtained a state of bliss that negated the careful conditioning they had undergone.

At the time of this incident in the early 1930s, no satisfactory explanation for this curious effect could be given. According to Mandell, however, subsequent research has not only allowed us to understand what happened but allows us to predict that this type of "ultraparadoxical response" would take place in the brain of many animals during a time of extreme stress or trauma—especially if the organism is near death. He points out that, under such circumstances, the organism can no longer function in a normal way and automatically switches to emergency processes, which, as we shall see, requires alteration of the chemistry and circuiting of the brain. If a crisis is sufficiently severe the hippocampus experiences the limits of its normal function. When the organism is first confronted with extreme stress, the neurocircuits are opened wider so that more and more information can be received. The evaluation process intensifies, as a solution to the present dilemma is sought; and the organism tries every response at its disposal that might conceivably be effective. But if no appropriate response can be found, that is, when absolute failure is inevitable, the organism responds with a new strategy—it gives up the battle and enters a state of tranquillity. Pavlov's hyperactive dogs, rescued just in the nick of time, had already given up trying to save themselves; they had given up functioning in a normal way, as a mentally active organism.

In this situation, according to Mandell, the hippocampus no longer functions as a mediator between the internal and external worlds. The internal circuit is amplified to the extent that it becomes the only source of information, the only reality, for the animal. Neuroscience explains that this amplification of the internal circuit and resulting masking of the external circuit is accomplished by a change in neurochemistry. Research has confirmed in many different experiments that, under conditions of severe stress, natural opiates are released in the brain. The effect of these opiates is to decrease the synthesis and release of the amine compound serotonin. And recent research has shown that the primary function of serotonin is to control the CA_3 triangular cells that are the mediator cells in the hippocampus's internal circuitry (399-401). It is a well-known principle of neuroscience that control is accomplished by inhibition of cell firing; that is, the details of neuroactivity are determined not by which cells are allowed to fire but by which cells are prevented from firing. So when the amount of serotonin in the hippocampus is reduced, the internal cells fire more rapidly. This increased activity amplifies the internal information and has the effect of masking the external information.

As in many other cases a small change in chemistry results in a rather radical change in consciousness, which is illustrated by the case of Pavlov's dogs. At one point the dogs must have suffered great trauma as they were confronted with an irresolvable life-threatening situation. But after their natural "escape button" had been pushed, that is, after being bathed in a rush of internal data that eclipsed the threatening external data, they achieved a state of bliss. Moreover it was found (and similar results have been confirmed many times) that the state of euphoria continued in the dogs even after they were removed from the traumatic situation. Mandell explains that this continuing effect is caused by a ''feed-forward'' characteristic of the CA_3 cells, which causes continuous firing and eventually exhausts many of the cells. If a sufficient number of these cells are not operable, the level of internal-circuit activity will remain high due to reduced inhibition, and a mild state of bliss will persist for some time (436). The dogs that had been carefully conditioned to be anxious and hyperactive were thus transformed through an encounter with death into calm and peaceful animals.

From Dogs to Humans—God in the Brain

According to Mandell, transcendent experience in human beings is analogous to the paradoxical experience of Pavlov's dogs. Because of the more highly evolved nature of the human brain, however, our experience is more complex. Unlike the dog's brain, the human's brain has a capacity for self-awareness; to some degree, it is aware of its own functioning. For example, a dog's brain performs the function of integrating the external and internal circuits and then of initiating responses based on the evaluation of information from these two contrasting neuroworlds. But the dog is not aware that this work is being done. People, however, are very much aware that they must be constantly comparing their needs and desires (presented to consciousness by the internal circuit) with the possibilities in the world for meeting those needs and desires (presented by the external circuit). As a matter of fact, most human mental activity is directed toward the task of seeing that needs are met within the restrictions given by the environment. From this point of view, human existence is always a struggle—a battle between self and other, with the knowledge that ultimately the self will lose. Underlying stress thus accompanies all human activity. But if a situation arises in which self is totally cut off from the other, this struggle can no longer occur. The self's struggle for survival can take place only when there is awareness of an external environment within which and over against which this struggle can take place. Hence, when the external circuit is effectively closed by the amplification of the internal circuit, there occurs an experience or peacefulness, calmness, or even euphoria and ecstasy (433).

In addition to feelings of peace or ecstasy, Mandell claims that one should also expect a considerable decrease, or even total loss, of the experience of self-consciousness or self-awareness. When the internal circuit is effectively operating alone, there is no need for the comparator or mediator function, and hence no need for the self as it is normally experienced. One might say that self-awareness becomes absorbed in the cloud of euphoria that accompanies the presence of highly amplified internal signals. Of course these circuits cannot function indefinitely in this state. Human existence is maintained by integrating internal and external information and by acting on the basis of this information. During the actual transcendent experience, however, there is a loss of awareness that these life-sustaining activities must be done. There is, rather, a sense that the battle has somehow been won (434-35).

Furthermore, when one asks, "What is the cause of this peace and joy?" the usual answers do not seem adequate. Either in reflecting on the experience afterward or even at times in understanding the transcendent experience while it is still occurring, one has the distinct awareness that it is being received rather than achieved. At the same time, this experience seems to be more true and more real than previous "normal" experiences. It is more true—even ultimately true—because with the loss of a sense of duality that accompanies this experience, there is no longer the possibility of conflict between alternatives that is part of all normal experiences (405). There is thus a sense of experiencing ultimate truth—truth beyond the duality of yes and no, right and wrong, valid and invalid. Again, it is more real, or even ultimately real, because, when the internal circuit is experienced in an amplified way, it appears to change its identity. Separated from external data to which it can normally be compared and in the absence of the necessity to perform the normal dualistic functions, the self appears to be something very different. It is certainly not the other, but it also does not appear to be the usual self. It is something so true that it has transcended the duality of knowledge and ignorance, so real that it has transcended the duality of life and death—even of being and nonbeing. It may thus be called the ultimate self, or Atman, or God. According to Mandell, then, when the transcendent experience occurs without the conscious intention of the individual, it is likely that the experience will be perceived as having been given to the individual by God (436).

Sources of Transcendent Experience

One would not expect a neuroscientist to take seriously the claim that God is both the source and the content of the transcendent experience. The actual source is whatever has caused the chemical changes that lead to the experience. Mandell discusses three ways by which transcendent experience may be triggered. In the first instance, transcendent experiences are often a part of certain neurological abnormalities. For example, it has long been known that seizures resulting from certain types of epilepsy are often accompanied by experiences of conversion or religious ecstasy. There is good but not yet conclusive evidence to support the belief that these "transcendent experiences" of epileptics are the result of chemical changes in the hippocampus (396-97). It is also known that patients with "bipolar affect disorders" often report ecstatic experience on "swing days." These patients undergo extreme alterations in mood from deep depression to hypermania. During the often brief periods when the switching is taking place, however, they routinely have experiences in which they claim great clarity of insight, a sense of imperturbability, and feelings of universal love and kindness. It is not uncommon for a patient in this swing phase to have extraordinary personal appeal and interpersonal charisma. Mandell notes that the clinical profile of these patients is strikingly similar to William James's description of "saintliness" and maintains that these bipolar experiences can be understood chemically in much the same way as the transcendent experiences described earlier (406).

Second, if one is not able to have a transcendent experience that results from neurological abnormality, one might choose a more controlled and voluntary path by ingesting the necessary chemicals. High doses of amphetamine, cocaine, certain hallucinogens, and cannabis can cause transcendent experiences. Although the exact chemical connection is not fully understood and although it is clear that these drugs affect many parts of the brain in addition to the hippocampus, Mandell is confident that the "pharmacological bridge" is sufficiently understood to say that the effect of these drugs are similar to, if not identical with, the results of the trauma suffered by Pavlov's dogs (386).

Finally, the most widely used method of inducing transcendent experience is through intentional stress. The great variety of spiritual disciplines practiced in the religious traditions of humankind have at least one thing in common—the intentional stressing of the organism. Each spiritual discipline calls upon its initiates to ask their bodies and brains to perform functions for which they are not normally adapted. Hatha yoga, fasting, and living burial all cause great physical stress; concentration, trying to answer an unanswerable question, endless repetition of a mantra, or detailed inspection of one's selfishness cause considerable mental stress. There seems to be an endless variety of spiritual discipline, but all induce stress in one way or another. The more vigorous the practice, the more severe the stress and the greater the likelihood of transcendent experience.

Mandell as Materialistic Reductionist

In the beginning of this discussion I referred to Mandell's position on the mind/brain problem as materialistic reductionism. I explain here why I believe this label is appropriate. For me, the first clue to Mandell's philosophy is revealed in his style. Every point in his lengthy discussion is carefully supported by copious references to technical research reported in prestigious psychological journals. (His bibliography contains over 400 items, and many of these are referred to a number of times.) For him, the keys to understanding the mind/brain are clearly to be found in the areas where psychology interfaces with the hard sciences. And even though there is no necessary connection between "hard scientific methodology" and an underlying materialistic reductionism, we are usually safe in associating the two.

One does not have to rely on style, however, to see the philosophy underlying Mandell's explanation of transcendent experience. For him, such experiences arise out of chemistry and not vice versa. His article indicates clearly that this transcendent experience is caused by a radical change in the normal function of the hippocampus due to the loss of the usual inhibiting action of the neurotransmitter serotonin. As we have seen, the weakening of serotonin inhibition can be accomplished in a number of ways— as a natural reaction to acute stress, as a by-product of certain neurological abnormalities, through the ingestion of certain chemicals, or as a neurological response to intentionally induced stress. In one sense the method of induction is incidental. If it is successful in effecting a change in chemistry in the brain, it will lead to transcendent experience—a change in mind. If the method does not change the chemistry, however, either because it is not of sufficient strength or rigor or perhaps because some other factors are blocking or canceling its chemical effect, the transcendent experience will not occur. Mandell does not speculate regarding the possibility that some paths to transcendence might not pass through the hippocampus, but his article leads one to conclude that he is convinced that any path can be explained by chemistry. For those who adopt this position, "God" is clearly present in the human brain. If the organism needs it—either to transform the trauma of dying into an experience of bliss or to escape the constant awareness that death is inevitable by entering a temporary state of trancendent ecstasy—the "God experience" is available. For Mandell, mind can understand how chemistry operates, but chemistry creates mind.

A MIDDLE POSITION:
TART AND A SYSTEMS APPROACH
TO UNDERSTANDING MIND/BRAIN

Charles Tart's "systems approach" offers an understanding of the relationship between mind and brain that represents a middle position between materialism and idealism. Tart is a professor of psychology at the University of California at Davis and is one of the leaders in the relatively new area of transpersonal psychology. Some of the primary differences between this school and that of traditional Western psychology will be apparent in the following discussion.

Definition of Terms

An explanation of Tart's theories must begin with the specialized terms he employs. Tart uses the term "brain" to refer to the physical organs of the neurosystem, in the same way as does orthodox psychology. He maintains, however, that knowledge of the brain established by studies such as the ones on which Mandell relies are not sufficient to explain human consciousness.[2] For him, "mind," "consciousness," and "awareness" are additional keys. He uses the term "mind" to refer to the "sum of all mental processes, actual or potential, of which the individual is capable" (28). The content of mind is thus determined to some extent by the external environment of the individual, since each environment will offer limited potential experience. Mind is also limited by the structures and function of the brain. For example, the human mind must operate (that is, experience must occur) within the limits allowed by what Tart calls the structures and subsystems of human consciousness. The subsystems are defined as follows:

1. *Exteroception*—the various means by which the sense organs register change from the environment (90).
2. *Interoception*—the various senses that tell us what is going on inside our bodies (93-94).
3. *Input processing*—"a complex, interlocking series of totally automatic processes" that compares data from interoceptors and exteroceptors against learned material stored in the memory; it accepts some incoming signals and lets others pass (97-98).
4. *Memory*—the capacity to store information from past experiences and to draw upon it in the present (104-105).
5. *Subconscious*—various mental processes or phenomena that occur outside awareness and of which we cannot normally become aware (109-14).
6. *Evaluation and decision making*—the intellectual cognitive processes with which we deliberately evaluate the meaning of things and decide what to do about them (114-15).
7. *Emotions*—feelings such as what we call grief, fear, joy, or surprise, which we can experience but which are difficult to define (124-25).
8. *Space/time sense*—the sense that events and experiences take place within a given spatial and temporal environment (125-26).
9. *Sense of identity*—the "ego sense," by which the assertion "this is me" or "this is mine" is attached to experience, memory, and action (129-36).

The structures of human consciousness are those more or less stable organizations of parts and pathways of the brain that make possible performance of certain functions. For example, the control of the heart is per-

---

[2]Charles Tart, *States of Consciousness* (El Cerrito CA: Psychological Process, 1983) 246-47. Hereafter in this section, page citations in the text refer to Tart's book.

formed by a given structure or set of interrelated structures. Such structures are fixed by biology and are not easily changed. Tart calls these kinds of structures the "hardware" of mental function (24). In contrast, the "software" structures are those that are determined by culture. For example, the ability to write results from the organization of a number of structures; and the ability to write English is the result of a more complex organization, which includes the writing structures as well as others related to understanding English. Function and structure are clearly closely related, but not identical. Different cultures and different individuals choose to activate certain structures or certain combinations of structures and do not activate others. These cultures and individuals are then able to perform only those functions related to the chosen structures, and in every case there are more structional organizations available than the few that are chosen. One of the most fascinating claims of transpersonal psychology is that the uniqueness of a culture, an individual, or a particular state of consciousness is determined by the structural software that is activated by that culture or individual or that is operational within a given state of consciousness. For Tart, the "mind" of an individual is the sum total of all experiences available to the individual, given the limits imposed by the way in which the subsystems of mental processes have been organized into workable structures and combinations of structures within that individual.

Although Tart sometimes uses the term "consciousness" to refer to a particular moment of mental life or a particular complex function of mind, for our purpose it will be useful to understand consciousness as he normally defines it, namely, as the union of mind with awareness (28). When mind presents a particular experience to awareness, consciousness results. This individual "moment of consciousness" should not be confused with a "state of consciousness"—a phrase by which Tart always means a unique configuration of psychological structures and subsystems (49-50).

A state of consciousness has a stable identity defined by a particular set of structures that holds the mind together and gives a sense of continuity to mental process. For example, what we call normal waking consciousness is a particular state of consciousness. It is one set of mental structures, one particular way of shaping experience, which has been given us by our individual neurology, by our culture, and, to some extent, by our own choice. Two other states of consciousness, the dream state and the state of dreamless sleep, are also experienced by all humans. Other states of consciousness, such as alcohol intoxication, are also readily available but may or may not be chosen. At any rate, when there is a change from one state of consciousness to another, this change has occurred because the configuration of psychological structures has been changed in such a way that experience is radically altered. Or to use a metaphor, a given state of consciousness is the particular filter that a given individual uses to sift reality. As the filter changes, either by choice or necessity, experience changes. For example, in a state of ordinary consciousness, one can experience the writing of English; in a state of dreamless sleep, one cannot. The configuration of a given state allows some experiences to occur but denies others. In a state of ordinary consciousness, one cannot experience levitation; in a dream state, one can. And as we shall see later, in the ordinary state of consciousness, one cannot experience transcendence; but in other states, one can.

Earlier I defined consciousness as a union of mind with awareness. And I have pointed out that, for Tart, mind is the totality of possible experience for an individual, given that individual's configuration of psychological structures, that is, given that individual's particular state of consciousness. Since "psychological structures" are just different ways in which the capacities of the brain are used, there is at this point no need to see consciousness as anything other than a product of the function of the brain. This is Mandell's position and is, according to Tart, the position of most psychologists. (He refers to this understanding as the conservative, or orthodox, interpretation [27-28].)

In his discussion of the nature of awareness, however, Tart intentionally separates himself and transpersonal psychology from the academic and scientific mainstream. He defines awareness as "the basic knowledge that something is happening to perceiving or feeling or cognizing in its simplest form" (27). In this definition there is nothing strange or radical; however, Tart further maintains that awareness is not a product or function of the brain. According to him there is too much evidence to the contrary— primarily from the witness of the spiritual traditions of the East and West, from scientific studies of parapsychological phenomena, and from his own and other scientific studies of altered states of consciousness—to continue to believe that awareness is a product or function of the brain. He is confident that awareness is independent of the brain. As a matter of fact, he calls his understanding of consciousness dualistic because it postulates the existence of two separate and independent substances. On the one hand, there is "mind," which in principle is reducible to brain and thus to matter; on the other hand, there is "awareness," which in principle is not reducible to matter (28-29).[3] He admits that very little can be said with

---

[3]See also Charles Tart, ed., *Transpersonal Psychologies* (New York: Harper & Row, 1975).

scientific certainty about the ultimate nature of awareness at this time; but he claims that the reason for this deficiency is that we have not (at least Western science has not) developed good techniques for studying awareness. He further suggests that, in order to understand awareness fully it might be necessary to choose to experience states of consciousness other than those with which we are now most familiar (31-32).

It is important to Tart to distinguish between self-awareness and pure awareness. Self-awareness is a product of brain. That is, as I am now aware that I am writing, that these are "my words," that this is "my paper" and "my pen," I am experiencing "self" or "ego" awareness. This self-awareness, or recognition that a particular entity is writing this paper, is similar to, though not identical with, the recognition that the writing is being done with a pen. Both experiences are the result of the functioning of certain psychological structures; that is, they are derived from specific operations of the brain.

Pure awareness, however, is not like self-awareness or "pen-awareness"; pure awareness is independent of the brain (158-59). In contrast to consciousness that is accompanied by self-awareness, a "Witness" or "Observer" consciousness is possible, according to Tart. When the Observer is activated, there is the awareness of mental activities without the association of those mental activities with the Observer. That is, the two elements of consciousness (mind and awareness) are split. The Observer, the source of awareness, is no longer identified with the experience being observed. According to Tart, not only is this dualism between the Observer and the observed possible, but the cultivation of this kind of consciousness may be a key to understanding both awareness and mind. For only from this Observer state can the operations of mind be objectively investigated. This state then might become a valuable tool for psychology (206-207).

A Systems Approach to Transcendence

Like Mandell, Tart insists that certain changes in ordinary consciousness have to take place in order for one to experience transcendence. Rather than focusing on the necessary chemical changes, however, Tart would have one look at the change in state of consciousness that would allow the experience to take place. For Tart, a state of consciousness is defined as the complex of psychological structures that are available to a person at a given time. The structures available to ordinary consciousness make the experience of nonduality impossible; for whereas this experience may be useful to spiritual growth or even to the study of awareness and mind, the experience is not useful to the everyday life of the living organism. By giving attention to the dualistic struggle for survival, the organism maintains itself within a sometimes hostile environment. It would therefore be expected that the destabilization of the ordinary state of consciousness, in which the experience of dualism is the norm, would be extremely difficult, since the very life of the organism would appear to be threatened. Although Tart believes that a state of consciousness in which transcendence would be a usual experience is possible, he does not explain in detail how the psychological structure of ordinary consciousness might be changed so that such a state would be established (229-30). My reading of Tart, however, suggests that something like the following would have to take place.

Changes in Exteroception. The fact that the information received by our senses from the external world is both persistent and fairly consistent is one of the strongest forces that binds attention to the ordinary state of consciousness. There appears to be an orderliness in the external world and a corresponding orderliness in our perception of it and our relationship to it. Because of this perceived orderly relationship, a certain comfort is derived from our ordinary interaction with the external world. If this order is radically disturbed, however, either because there has been a critical change in the external environment or, what is more likely, an alteration in the way the senses are allowed to operate, the ordinary state of consciousness tends to be destabilized, and the individual will experience strangeness, or a sense of disorientation or even physical nausea. Tart points out that there are three ways in which the function of the senses can be altered: deprivation, overloading, and confusion of patterns (91-93). If stimulation of the senses is radically reduced, one no longer has the persistent reinforcement of a consistent external world, and a sense of loss results. Similarly, a feeling of emptiness or confusion may result if the senses are saturated with strong stimuli—at a rock concert, for example, where the normal sense of orderly relationship is disturbed. In either case there is a tendency for the ordinary state to be destabilized.

Another means of destabilizing consciousness is through a forced change in the pattern or structure of stimuli. Looking at a surrealist painting or an Escher print or listening to atonal, arhythmic sounds of certain contemporary music is disturbing to many people. It has also been discovered that, if the normal functioning of a person's eyes is altered by forcing one to view the same spot for a period of time, all sorts of unusual perceptual changes take place (93). What is perceived to be a very orderly relationship between the external world and consciousness can be rather easily disturbed, and any persistent disturbances tend to destabilize the ordinary state.

Changes in Interoception. Everyone destabilizes the ordinary state of consciousness by changing the patterns of stimulation from the body. In passing from alertness to sleeping or dreaming, one passes from one state of consciousness to another. One of the means of effecting the change is by lying down and relaxing the body, which alters the normal pattern of interoception. Each of us has a certain "body image"—that is, interoceptive experience of our body—that we believe to be persistent through time, and an alteration of that body image can lead to a change in consciousness. If sensations from the body are either extremely pleasant or extremely painful, as in the case of certain types of spiritual discipline (for example, fasting, exhaustive dancing, forcing the body to hold certain positions [mudras] for a long period of time, or altering the normal balance of the body with a "witch's cradle" device), the ordinary state of consciousness tends to break down (96).

Changes in Input Processing. We have already seen in our discussion of Mandell that a change of consciousness can be accomplished by a radical alteration of normal input processing. Tart maintains, however, that the flooding of the input processing subsystem with interoception and the resulting masking of exteroception is only one way in which this subsystem could be altered in order to bring about a change in consciousness. He points out that the input processing complex receives information from at least four sources: exteroception, interoception, memory, and the subconscious. One of the functions of input processing is to differentiate carefully among the signals from each of the areas. The failure of input processing to make these distinctions causes considerable confusion among separate flows of information and radically alters perception. For example, almost everyone has had a déjà vu experience; in most cases, the experiences causes a sense of strangeness and disorientation, that is, destabilization. Tart explains such experience as the momentary failure of input processing to distinguish between information coming from the senses and information coming from the memory. Normally the input processing system will label each input carefully. In this case, though, the individual is not sure whether he or she is seeing something or is remembering something (108-109, 127-29).

If the momentary experience of déjà vu is disturbing to ordinary consciousness, it would not be surprising to learn that a more radical and persistent change in the input processing system would completely alter consciousness. For example, let us suppose that the usual distinctions between the four kinds of information received by input processing were not made. This condition would result in the conviction that information from the external world, information from the body (including other parts of the brain), information from the memory, and information from the subconscious were coming from the same source. All information coming to input processing would be treated with "equanimity"—a favorite word of seers and mystics. And such an experience would not only tend to disturb ordinary consciousness, it would also be similar to, if not identical with, the experience of transcendence.

Changes in Memory, Emotion, and the Subconscious. In order to explain Tart's understanding of the nature of consciousness, it is not necessary to discuss these three independent subsystems separately. He says essentially the same thing about all three, namely, that any radical change in their functions can destabilize the ordinary state and in some cases induce a different state. If for one reason or another consciousness were dominated by either of these subsystems—that is, if awareness were focused exclusively on one of these—an altered state would be the result. Tart maintains that a strong emotional state, such as when one is enraged, overcome by grief, or extremely anxious or frightened, should be regarded as a different state of consciousness (124-25). And just as the emotions can capture consciousness, so one can become "lost in memory" or overcome by subsconscious impulses to the extent that consciousness is altered. On the other hand, a severe restriction of the information from any one or all of these subsystems would also tend to destabilize the ordinary state (106-10).

Changes in Evaluation and Decision Making. The primary function of the input processing subsystem is to present a clear and distinct image to awareness. Under normal circumstances input processing receives information and identifies the source of the information. For example, it may recognize that certain information coming from the senses has its source in a tree and would then present to awareness the image of a tree. In this way input processing identifies objects. And once a complex of information is identified, it must be evaluated and responded to if a response is considered necessary. The assigning of meaning and value and the choice of an appropriate response are the functions of what Tart calls appropriately the evaluation and decision-making subsystem.

Tart's research has convinced him that every state of consciousness has its own particular way of assigning value and meaning, and thus its own particular way of making decisions about the appropriateness of a given response. Or as he likes to say, every state of consciousness has its own system of reasoning—its own particular logic (114-23). For example, the normal state of consciousness is controlled by a dualistic system of reason. This system of reason is based on three fundamental principles: the self is different from the other, the self is the center of value, and the meaning that the self assigns to the other is the true meaning of the other. When this system is controlling awareness, the image of the tree that is presented by input processing will always be identified as something other than the self that identifies it as "tree." The meaning of the tree will be identified as the meaning understood by the self, and the value of the tree will be determined by the relationship of the tree to the self. This system of reasoning is obviously very useful in helping to sustain the life of the individual within its environment.

A different state of consciousness would require a different system of reasoning, a different logic. For example, a nondualistic state of consciousness might be based on the fundamental principle that the self is nondifferent from the other, that the value of a thing is based on its relationship to all things, and that the meaning of something is determined by the nature of its relationships to other things. A state of consciousness with these or similar principles controlling its evaluation and decision-making processes would certainly be different from what we call the normal state of consciousness. According to Tart, the usual judgment that the ordinary state is superior to other states is an expected conclusion of ordinary-state evaluation. He maintains that any state that includes evaluation would judge itself to be superior to other states (121).

Changes in Sense of Identity. A clear sense of identity is very important to ordinary consciousness. In sleeping, this sense is completely lost; in dreaming, it is sometimes confused. The stability of ego identification is thus a pillar of the ordinary state of consciousness, just as is a given system of logic. As a matter of fact, one of the reasons for strong resistance to the destabilization of the ordinary state is that destabilization often is accompanied by a loss of self-identity. "Self" or "ego" is perceived to be identical with the ordinary state of consciousness. A sense of identity, however, need not be a part of a state of consciousness. I have already mentioned Tart's concept of the Witness or Observer state. In the Witness state there is awareness; that is, there is the knowledge that experience is occurring as usual, but there is no awareness that a "self" is participating in the experience. There is pure awareness without the sense that there is one who is aware (159-60). The sense of identity of a person in a transcendent state would obviously be rather different from one who perceives oneself to be experiencing a normal state of consciousness.

Changes in Space/Time Sense. According to Tart, our sense of space and time is similar to our sense of logic and of self-identity in that it is a part of a given state of consciousness rather than an objective reality that cannot be altered (125-29). He maintains, in fact, that our particular perception of the nature of space and time is bound very closely to our particular sense of identity. Space to us is the space in which the self operates; and time is the past, present, and future of the self. If our sense of self-identity changed, we would also experience a change of space/time. Of course the converse would also be true. All of us are aware that perceptions of space and time are altered somewhat in dream consciousness, where one frequently experiences simultaneous events that in normal consciousness happened at different times and in different places. And persons who have experienced alcohol or drug intoxication frequently report an altered perception of space and time. Our normal understanding divides both space and time into consistent increments, which we accept as absolute. Furthermore, we understand space to be determined by three dimensions and time by one. In a different state of consciousness, space and time would not necessarily have these particular characteristics. As a matter of fact, a sense of space and time would not even have to be present in order for a state of consciousness to be self-consistent.

Effects on Motor Output. The culmination of normal psychological processes is response. All the processing of information—classification, identification, understanding, and evaluation—is done for the purpose of making appropriate response. To the ordinary state the appropriate response is one that will in some way support the health and happiness of the self. In a different state of consciousness, the appropriate response may be very different. For example, to a nondualistic state of consciousness an appropriate response would be one that would tend to preserve the health and happiness of all beings. The same love and concern that ordinary consciousness expresses for the self, nondual consciousness would tend to express for all beings, since there is no duality between the responding self and the other toward which the response is made. The Hindu practice of ahisma or the bodhisattva's vow to "dedicate the next ten thousand lives to all sentient beings" or Jesus' command to love others as one loves oneself makes more sense to nondual consciousness than to dual consciousness.

Tart as a Realist

I call Tart's position realism, the philosophical school that for me stands between idealism and materialism. With the materialists, Tart affirms the ultimate reality of matter. According to him, consciousness is dependent on the structures of the brain. But with the idealists, Tart affirms the ultimate reality of a nonmaterial entity that he calls awareness. He acknowledges his break with orthodox psychology by maintaining that awareness is not a product of the brain, not just a function of conscious mind. He is convinced that awareness is autonomous, that it comes from outside the brain. Furthermore, he implies, or at least appears to suggest, that awareness has some freedom to choose the type of consciousness in which it will participate. According to Tart, the structure of the brain interacts with awareness to create both semistable states of consciousness and moments of conscious awareness; in doing so, brain affects awareness, but awareness also affects brain (27-32).

A VIEW FROM ABOVE:
KARL PRIBRAM AS IDEALIST

Karl Pribram, professor of psychology at Stanford, began his research under the direction of Karl Lashley at the Yerkes Laboratories. Lashley, following Sherrington and the stimulus-response approach to psychology, believed that the memory of a given object or event is stored in a particular nerve cell or small group of cells. Thirty years of research, however, failed to establish this "memory in a cell" or "engram" theory of brain operation. In response to this failure to confirm stimulus-response theory, Pribram set out on his own and in 1971 published *Languages in the Brain,* in which he proposed a neurological theory so radically different from current thought that some have called it the beginning of a paradigm shift in neuroscience.[4]

Pribram's writing is highly technical and complex, at times to the point of obscurity. Rather than try to summarize his theory, I will give a general description of what he thinks happens when the operation of seeing and identifying an object is performed by the human neurosystem. The operation can be divided into four functions: focusing by the lens, transformation by the retina, transmission to appropriate areas of the brain for recording, and recognition.

Visual Focus as a Subjective Act

When the eyelids are opened, the eye is confronted with light waves that come from several different objects. Only one of these objects, however, can be seen at a given time. The process by which the light waves from a given object are selected over others and passed to the retina we call focusing. Although a proper focus is accomplished by subtle changes in the lens, many other parts of the optical system contribute to this operation. Pribram maintains that it is important to remember that the lens is guided in its focusing movements by information it receives from other optical areas. The total optical system is involved in selecting the light waves that are to be received. Through this process of selection the system is able to isolate the chosen object from its environment and present the reality of a separate entity to consciousness. Light waves do not arrive at the eye with labels that identify the object from which they come. The lens, with help

---

[4]See K. Wilber, ed., *The Holographic Paradigm* (Boulder CO: Shambhala Publications, 1982).

from other optical areas, must accomplish this complicated task. In a sense, then, the optical system creates the object that is to be presented to consciousness by this process of selective focus. This choice to receive certain light waves while rejecting all others is part of what I am calling the subjectivity of the process of seeing. Because of the complexity of the optical system and the constant interaction among the various parts of the system during any operation, no two optical systems will perform in exactly the same way. The same could be said for any other sensory system. As a matter of fact, the performance of a particular system will vary from time to time, depending on the mental state of the individual (116-39).[5]

The Retina as Neurotransformer

Pribram has concentrated a great deal of his own research on the operation of the retina. As a result he concludes that the retina is a transformer rather than a transmitter of information. Light comes to the eye in wave form, but the wave patterns are temporarily lost when the light is focused. Surprisingly, however, research has demonstrated that the retina, working in a complex way through multiple connections among its cells and various cell layers as it performs millions of operations in a few microseconds, actually transforms the information it receives back into wave patterns. Hence, according to Pribram, optical information should be thought of as a complex of waves rather than a collection of impulses. He claims that the neurosystem is a receiver, transmitter, transformer, and creator of wave patterns; the interaction of these wave patterns constitutes much neuroactivity. The light waves that strike the lens cannot interact directly with the wave patterns already present in the brain; hence, they must be transformed in such a way that a matching, or resonance, can take place. This transformation is accomplished by the retina, with the aid of constant feedback from other parts of the optical system (54-65).

The Wave Nature of Neuromotion

After information has been transformed by the retina, it moves into other optical areas as a complex of wave patterns. One wave pattern is created by the interaction of the nerve cells that are activated by a given transformation. Earlier theories claimed that learning and memory took place through the interactions among, and changes within, these neurons. These theories, however, were confronted with two major dilemmas. Very early

---

[5]Karl Pribram, *Languages of the Brain* (Englewood Cliffs NJ: Prentice-Hall, 1971) 116-39. Hereafter in this section, page citations in the text refer to Pribram's work.

in neuroscience it was learned that the number of neurons in the brain and the structural relationship among these neurons remained essentially the same throughout life. If no substantial change could be made in the number of cells or structure of the brain-cell network, how could learning and memory be accomplished? It was concluded that learning must take place through changes within the individual cells.

For years Lashley and others of the stimulus-response school sought evidence to prove this hypothesis. As previously mentioned, however, this research ended in failure. If learning takes place via the changes in the internal structures of a neuron, then that particular neuron is the site of that particular piece of information. If that cell is lost or damaged, that information would be lost or distorted. Such a model is easy to test. One could teach an animal a simple new behavior. Then one could isolate the cell or group of cells where the information about that behavior was stored. When the cell or cells involved were removed, the learned behavior would be forgotten, and the animal would be unable to perform the operation. The research procedure was straightforward, but the results were devastating to the theoretical proposition that learning took place in the brain cells. It was found that, even after large areas of the brain were removed, a conditioned animal could still perform the learned activity. Try as they might, researchers could not locate the cell or cells in which learned information was stored. As a matter of fact, it became clear that learning takes place within large areas of the brain. Information appears to be stored in several places rather than in one. These results understandably caused great consternation among neuroscientists of the behaviorist school (26).

Pribram's wave model of mind/brain operation offers a solution to this problem. In addition to the impulse waves that are propagated along neuropathways through the interactions among neurons, there is, according to Pribram, a second wave field that always accompanies the first and that is perpendicular to it in the same way that a magnetic field is always present in the area surrounding an electric circuit. As this wave field moves through the active area of the brain, it interacts with the neuromicrostructure (9-25).

At this point it is necessary to digress for a moment to explain what is meant by neuromicrostructure. As I have stated, brain research prior to Pribram focused on the understanding of cells or even larger systems. But Pribram, with the aid of new research equipment and technique, focuses attention on the fine structure of the brain. He maintains that the structure significant to learning and memory is that which is formed by the connections between the cell fibers rather than the connections between the cell nuclei. Each nerve cell has hundreds or even thousands of branch fibers that make contact with the fibers of other cells to form a very complex matrix. This matrix Pribram calls the microstructure of the brain. He maintains that it is this fibrous microstructure matrix, rather than the cell matrix, that is changed in the process of learning (26-47).

Learning and Memory as Wave Resonance

When a wave field is introduced into appropriate areas of the brain, one of two things can happen. If the wave field contains information about a familiar object, a matching (or resonance) will be established between the wave field and the existing microstructure. When this resonance has been fixed, the brain has completed the task of "seeing the object." The recognition that this particular object is an apple and the recollection of other memories associated with "apple" in a given brain are also accomplished by the resonance that is achieved by the interaction of secondary wave fields with other parts of the brain's microstructure. Recognition and memory are thus the result of a number of different resonances that occur in different parts of the brain (101-15).

If the incoming wave field contains information about an unfamiliar object, recognition cannot occur. If the information is considered significant enough so that the neurosystem persists in its presentation, however, changes will be made in the microstructure of appropriate areas of the brain. These changes will continue until resonance with the coming wave information is achieved. When this process is finished, learning has taken place. Physiologically, learning is thus accomplished by making changes in the connections between cell fibers. In support of Pribram's theory, research has shown that, whereas nerve cells do not change, nerve cell fibers do easily and frequently change in length and thickness, especially during the early years when most learning is taking place (271-90).

Before leaving this section, I would like to explain how Pribram's wave model solves the problem with which neuroscience has been confronted since it was learned that memory was spread over large areas of the brain. The earlier theories assumed that information was stored in the brain in much the same way that information is stored in a computer. Pribram, however, has forsaken the computer analogy for a hologram analogy, maintaining that information is stored in the brain in a way similar to the what it is stored on a holographic plate. Holography is a special kind of photography that has only recently been understood and explored.[6] An interesting feature of holography is that the images it produces are three-dimensional and quite lifelike in many ways. If the brain stores information in a way analogous to holography, it is no surprise that,

---

[6]W. K. Koch, *Lasers and Holography* (New York: Doubleday, 1969).

even with our eyes closed, we can "see"three-dimensional, lifelike images. The most important characteristic of holography to Pribram is the manner in which information is stored on the exposed plate. Unlike a regular photograph, a hologram is made without a lens to focus the light. Information about every part of the object is thus stored on every part of the hologram. If the complete hologram is exposed, a single image will appear. But if the holograph is broken into several pieces and each of these pieces is then exposed in the prescribed way, each piece of the hologram, no matter how small, will produce an image of the entire object.

If, as Pribram claims, information storage in the microstructure of the brain is analogous to information storage in a hologram, then it is not difficult to understand why memory is unaffected by the removal of parts of the brain. Removal of part of the brain is analogous to removal of parts of the holography, which does not appreciably affect the reproduction of the holographic image. By postulating that neuroactivity is wavelike as well as circuitlike, Pribram is thus able to explain neurophenomena that have been highly problematic to other theories (140-66).

Self-Image and Microstructure Resonance

If the processes described above as recognition and learning (along with many other neuroprocesses that have not been described here) are carried out smoothly, the individual experiences a feeling of competence. To varying degrees, depending on the complexity and perceived urgency of the task, our sense of self-worth is determined by how effective we are at achieving resonance in our neuroprocesses. If wave patterns coming from the external world or from parts of our body are easily matched—that is, are "understood"—we are content. But if this process is not completed, we are anxious. Because of this relationship between the ability to achieve resonance and the evaluation of self, there is always a vested interest in maintaining a stable environment—both external and internal. Change is necessary to life and growth, but change also threatens the self (252-71).

Pribram's Wave Model
and Transcendent Consciousness

In *Languages of the Brain* there is no discussion of mystical or transcendent experience. There Pribram describes "normal" experience, using a revolutionary model of the mind/brain. In the decade following the publication of his technical work, however, he became interested in understanding the philosophical implications of his theory. In collaboration with David Bohm, a theoretical physicist who was a colleague of Einstein's at the Institute for Advanced Studies, the wave model of mind/brain has been expanded and integrated into a general wave theory of reality. This Pribram-Bohm theory, though based on data from both contemporary physics and psychology, is obviously compatible with the traditions of idealism in both Eastern and Western mystical traditions. The theory maintains that ultimate or primary reality is wavelike in nature and that all images, emotions, and words are mere secondary or derived reality. It claims further that all secondary realities are hologramlike projections from a dimension of primary reality that transcends space and time and materiality and that does not interact with ordinary consciousness.[7]

According to this idealistic view of reality, a transcendent experience would result whenever direct interaction between an individual wave field (a mind/brain) and the wave field of primary reality occurred. Ordinary experience is always indirect. As mentioned above, in Pribram's description of ordinary neurooperations, several steps must occur in order for an individual to experience an object in the ordinary way. First, the object must have physical properties that allow it to transform light waves in such a way as to cause them to be propagated to the eye. The light waves are then transformed into a beam by the lens in the process of focusing. In the retina another complex process occurs in which the beam of light is transformed back into a wave pattern, which has properties that enable it to interact with the microstructure of the individual mind/brain. Finally, the experience of the object is recorded in a hologramlike image in the microstructure. Only after these complex operations is the object "seen."

It might be possible under certain conditions, however, to experience the reality of the object directly, that is, for the wave field of the object to interact directly with the wave field of the individual mind/brain. According to contemporary physical theory, every object can be thought of as a complex of waves that can be described mathematically in detail through the use of Schrödinger's equation. Furthermore, the wave reality of an object has the property of being extended, at least potentially, through all space. As we have seen, Pribram suggests that the individual mind/brain also has a wave component, which I have been calling the wave field. Theoretically, this wave field is not contained in the space occupied by the brain. It extends throughout space in the same way as does a magnetic field.

From this point of view, the wave field of the individual and the wave field of the object are thus in constant contact, at least potentially. If the individual could become aware of this contact or, to put it another way, if resonance could be achieved between the two wave fields and could be recognized in some way, a radically different kind of experience, one that

---

[7]Wilber, *Holographic Paradigm*, 22.

might be called transcendent, would have occurred. Accompanying this experience would be a sense of unity or even identity of self with the object, since resonance between wave fields can occur only when the wave patterns are compatible or essentially alike and since resonance is an intermingling or unity of wave fields. In this direct experience one might expect that there would be no sense of difference between two wave fields.

If one believes that such experiences are possible—and according to the Pribram-Bohm theory, they are—one might ask the question, "Why are such experiences not occurring continually?" According to the theory, the wave field of the individual is potentially in contact with the wave fields of all other realities. If this contact can be recognized, why is it not always, or at least frequently, recognized? The answer to this question is that the individual mind/brain is not usually aware of its direct contact with primary reality because it is constantly occupied with its indirect interaction with secondary reality. As was pointed out earlier, the individual self is usually experienced as being that which is able to perform effectively the complex operations that allow the indirect experience to occur. Self-identity and self-worth are inexorably integrated with the functions of normal consciousness. The experience of the loss of these functions appears to be the same as the experience of the death of the self. In one sense it is fear that tenaciously binds the attention to the processes of ordinary consciousness. It is therefore not surprising that all spiritual traditions insist that, in order for transcendent experience to occur, the ordinary sense of self-identity must be either surrendered or destroyed. When the self as normally understood is set aside, that is, when the attention of consciousness is turned away from the ordinary operations of indirect experience, direct experience can occur.

PRAJAPATI'S VIEW—AN INTEGRATION OF THREE MODELS

In this chapter I have given a necessarily brief and admittedly simplistic description of three different models of mind/brain and have suggested how each of these models could be used to understand the meaning of transcendent experience. Following the example of Prajapati, the supreme Vedic god, in the final chapter of the Chhandogya *Upanishad,* I suggest that there is no need to choose among these three models—each can be useful in its own way.[8]

In the Chhandogya we are told the story of how Indra, the representative of the gods, and Virochana, the representative of the demons, went to Prajapati and asked him to explain to them the true nature of the self.

---

[8]Nikhilananda, *The Upanishads* (New York: Harper & Row, 1963).

Prajapati told them that the self is that which can be seen as a reflection in water—a body, a physical being that exists for a time and then passes away. This is the self of everyday experience, the self of "waking consciousness" that one identifies as the source of one's thoughts, feelings, and actions. At first both representatives appeared to be pleased with the explanation and left to return to their respective domains. Virochana went back to the demons and told them that the self is the same as the body. The demons were pleased. If they wish to understand the meaning of transcendent experience, it would thus be appropriate for them to use a model of brain/mind similar to Mandell's. Models of this kind are most useful in helping one to understand the material nature of the self and the materialistic meaning of religious experience. Such models, however, are limited in their usefulness.

Although Indra at first accepted this answer, a little reflection on its meaning convinced him that it was not completely adequate. He returned to Prajapati for further instruction. This time Indra was told that the self is that which experiences dreams—at times involved in the dream and at other times merely the observer of the dream. The "dream self" is sometimes material and sometimes not; at times it is active, and at other times it is the observer of the action. This self is always associated with a body—either as actor or as observer of action. It is never completely free from body and never completely identical with body. This is the self that can move from action to action, from experience to experience, from body to body, without itself being changed. This self is limited in space, because it is always associated with a particular body; but it is not limited in time, because it moves eternally from body to body.

If one wishes to understand this dimension of the self, it would be appropriate to use a model of mind/brain similar to the one proposed by Tart. Tart's model is grounded in materialistic research; but because he insists that awareness, a necessary component of consciousness, is nonmaterial, his model allows one to explain how consciousness (self) can shift from one state to another, or from one body (which represents a particular set of potential states) to another body. This model should thus be useful to one who wishes to understand the meaning of self as a combination of material and nonmaterial—as a soul or jiva. But this understanding of self and this kind of model also has limits.

As the story continues, we are told that Indra was not completely satisfied with this second explanation, so he returned again to Prajapati. This time he was told that the self is to be identified with dreamless sleep. This self is completely free from material existence; it is limited by neither time nor space. It is often described as both universal and eternal, but it is realized that even these descriptions are not completely adequate. This self, which in the Hindu tradition is called Atman, cannot be properly understood by any model; a model of mind/brain such as the one proposed by Pribram, however, which suggests that reality is nonmaterial or wavelike rather than material or particlelike, is clearly more appropriate than others.[9]

Finally, we are told that Indra was not completely satisfied with this identification of self with the one who experiences the complete freedom from material existence that is analogous to dreamless sleep. He returned to his teacher for one last time. Prajapati's final remarks are sufficiently ambiguous to allow a number of different interpretations, but I prefer the interpretation that claims a partial truth for all three of the previous answers but denies complete or ultimate truth to any single limited answer. Following Prajapati's advice, I suggest that each of the models of mind/brain here discussed can be useful in helping one understand the meaning of transcendent experience, but I suggest further that any conclusions based only on any one of these models will be both partially true and partially false. Mandell's model understands the self to be material, and Pribram's model allows for a totally nonmaterial understanding of the self. Used together, they lead one toward a complete understanding of self and of transcendent experience.

---

[9]The contributors to Wilber, *Holographic Paradigm,* certainly reach such a conclusion.

References

Mandell

Adey, W. R. 1964. "Computer Analysis of Hippocampal EEG Activity and Impedance in Approach Learning: Effects of Psychotomimetic and Hallucinogenic Drugs." In *Pharmacology of Conditioning, Learning, and Retention*. New York: Academic Press.

Aghajanian, G. K. and B. W. Bunney. 1973. "Central Dopaminergic Neurons: Neurophysiological Identification and Response to Drugs." In E. Usdin and S. H. Snyder, eds., *Frontiers in Catecholamine Research*. Oxford: Pergamon.

Allison, G. E. 1967. "Psychiatric Implications of Religious Conversion." *Canadian Psychiatric Association Journal* 12:55-61.

Anderson, P. and T. Lomo. 1970. "Mode of Control of Hippocampal Pyramidal Cell Discharges." In R. Whelan, ed., *The Neural Control of Behavior*. New York: Academic.

Barchas, J. and E. Usdin, eds. 1973. *Serotonin and Behavior*. New York: Academic.

Bunney, W. E., F. K. Goodwin, and D. L. Murphy. 1972. "The 'Switch Process' in Manic-Depressive Illness." *Archives of General Psychiatry* 27:312-17.

Chadoff, P. and H. Lyons. 1958. "Hysteria—the Hysterical Personality in Hysterical Conversion." *American Journal of Psychiatry* 114:734-70.

Christensen, C. W. 1963. "Religious Conversion." *Archives of General Psychiatry* 9:207-16.

Davidson, J. and R. Davidson, eds. 1980. *The Psychobiology of Consciousness*. New York: Plenum Press.

Dean, S. R., ed. 1975. *Psychiatry and Mysticism*. New York: Nelson-Hall.

Dewhurst, K. and A. W. Beard. 1970. "Sudden Religious Conversion in Temporal Lobe Epilepsy." *British Journal of Psychiatry* 117:497-507.

Horton, P. C. 1974. "The Mystical Experience: Substance of an Illusion." *Journal of the American Psychoanalytic Association* 22:364-80.

Isaacson, R. and K. Pribram, eds. 1975. *The Hippocampus*. 2 vols. New York: Plenum.

Knook, H. L. 1966. *The Fibre-Connections of the Forebrain*. Philadelphia: Davis.

Mandell, A. J. 1978. "The Neurochemistry of Religious Insight and Ecstasy." In K. Berrin, ed., *Art of the Huichol Indians*. New York: Abrams.

——————. 1980. "Toward a Psychobiology of Transcendence: God in the Brain." In Julian Davidson and Richard Davidson, eds., *The Psychobiology of Consciousness*. New York: Plenum Press.

Mandell, A. J. and S. Knapp. 1977. "Regulation of Serotonin Biosynthesis in the Brain." *Federation Proceedings* 36:2142-48.

Pahnke, W. N. 1966. "Drugs and Mysticism." *International Journal of Parapsychology* 8:257-94.

Pavlov, I. P. 1933. *"Les sentiments d'emprise* and the Ultraparadoxical Phase." *Journal de Physiologie* 30:9-10.

Sargant, W. 1969. "The Physiology of Faith." *British Journal of Psychiatry* 115:505-18.

Sedman, D. and G. Hopkinson. 1966. "The Psychopathology of Mystical and Religious Conversion in Psychiatric Patients." *Confinia Neurologia* 9:1-19, 65-77.

Segal, M. 1975. "Physiological and Pharmacological Evidence for a Serotonergic Projection to the Hippocampus." *Brain Research* 94:115-31.

Wallace, R. K. and H. Benson. 1972. "The Physiology of Meditation." *Scientific American* 226:84-90.

Tart

Deikman, A. 1966. "De-automatization and the Mystic Experience." *Psychiatry* 29:329-43.

Goleman, D. 1972. "The Buddha on Meditation and States of Consciousness." *Journal of Transpersonal Psychology* 4(1):1-44.

Green, E. A. Green, and E. Walters. 1970. "Voluntary Control of Internal States." *Journal of Transpersonal Psychology* 2(1):1-26.

Masters, R. and J. Houston. 1971. *The Altered States of Consciousness Induction Device: Some Possible Uses in Research and Psychotherapy.* Pomona NY: Foundation for Mind Research.

Naranjo, C. and R. Ornstein. 1971. *On the Psychology of Meditation.* New York: Viking.

Tart, C. 1972. "States of Consciousness and State-specific Sciences." *Science* 176:1203-10.

_____1983. *States of Consciousness.* New York: Harper & Row.

_____, ed. 1969. *Altered States of Consciousness.* New York: Wiley.

_____1975. *Transpersonal Psychologies.* New York: Harper & Row.

Timmons, B. and J. Kamiya. 1970. "The Psychology and Physiology of Meditation and Related Phenomena: A Bibliography." *Journal of Transpersonal Psychology* 2:41-59.

Timmons. B. and D. Kanellakos. 1970. "The Psychology and Physiology of Meditation and Related Phenomena: Bibliography II." *Journal of Transpersonal Psychology* 6:32-38.

Pribram

Bohm, D. 1971. "Quantum Theory as an Indication of a New Order in Physics. Part A: The Development of New Orders as Shown through the History of Physics." *Foundations of Physics* 1(4):359-81.

_____. 1973. "Quantum Theory as an Indication of a New Order in Physics. Part B: Implicate and Explicate Order in Physical Law." *Foundations of Physics* 3(2):139-68.

Bohr, N. 1958. *Atomic Physics and Human Knowledge.* New York: Wiley.

Pribram, K. 1969. "Neurophysiology of Remembering." *Scientific American* 221:73-86.

_____. 1971. *Languages of the Brain.* Englewood Cliffs NJ: Prentice-Hall.

_____. 1977. "Holonomy and Structure in the Organization of Perception." *Proceedings of the Conference on Images, Perception, and Knowledge.* University of Western Ontario.

Wilber, Ken, ed. 1982. *The Holographic Paradigm.* Boulder CO: Shambhala Publications.

A NEUROPSYCHOLOGICAL COMMENTARY ON BIBLICAL FAITH

Frank B. Wood

Biblical faith, in my view here, is the faith of the Old, as well as of the New Testament, and it is the faith of Jews and Christians around the world. It is not to be understood generally as religious faith, but only as the religious faith of the Bible. This commentary on it is but one limited expression of its partial content; it dissects out a few states of mind that are also states of brain and comments on their significance for biblical faith. There is a debate these days about what religion is and what kind of mental experiences it calls for; in entering that debate, I will not attempt to say that the Jewish or the Christian faith is limited to the particular states of mind and brain I discuss. It has always been uniquely true of biblical faith that it has found itself expressible in a variety of media and through a variety of thought systems. The purpose of this particular proposal is to consider the expression in neuropsychological terms, without implying that these are the only ways or even the best ways it can or should be expressed.

With such preliminary provisos out of the way, let me state my thesis plainly. In contrast to a large variety of current literature from the sophisticated to the popular—all of which claims that there is something specifically gestalt, intuitive, holistic, nonverbal, and right-hemispheric about religious experience—I maintain that the faith we have presented in the

Bible is actually a verbal, sequential, analytical, particularized, and therefore left-hemispheric mode of thinking.

It is obvious that the faith of the Bible is verbal. It says so in the plainest terms. The God of the Bible insists that no pictures be made of him. He insists, instead, that he be listened to, that he be obeyed, not that he be experienced or felt, least of all that he be seen or pictured. There is no greater sin in the Old Testament than the sin of making pictures of God. Likewise in the New Testament, the familiar prologue to John's Gospel states that the original reality is Word. All things were made by this Word; without this Word was not anything made that was made; this Word became flesh and dwelt among us, full of grace and truth, and we beheld its glory, says John, glory as of the only begotten Son of the Father. This is Word, address, or summons, but not picture, not experience, not intuition, not gestalt.

Let us consider certain correlations or implications from this fact of the verbal nature of biblical faith that may enrich and add meaning to its context. If I say that the religion of the Bible is verbal in large measure, then contemporary neuroscience will derive implications that would confirm the essential verbal character of the faith. Moreover, in drawing implications from contemporary neuroscientific understanding of the brain and the mind, we may fill out and enrich our understanding of the kind of experience that is set forth in the New Testament and in the Old Testament.

If the faith of the Bible is verbal, then it should be oriented toward the emotions and cognitions of approach. There is an emerging understanding in the contemporary neuroscientific community that the left hemisphere is the verbal hemisphere because of its emotional tone. It is the hemisphere of language because it is the hemisphere of approach behavior. This fact can be demonstrated in a variety of ways, one of the most interesting of which relates to the neurochemistry of the left and right hemispheres. Studies of humans and animals have yielded increasing evidence of a neurotransmitter, dopamine, that is represented in greater proportion in the left hemisphere than in the right. It is not a huge part of the left brain's activity, but it does seem to be heavily involved in controlling and modulating its activity. It would be interesting for us to remember whence it comes evolutionarily. Evolutionarily, this little control system within the brain is all tangled up with the sense of olfaction. It is by evolutionary heritage the regulator of behavior as that behavior is signaled by a sense of smell. This function contrasts with a corresponding neurotransmitter, norepinephrine, that is more heavily represented in the right hemispheres and more enmeshed in the evolutionary history of the sense of taste. The differences between the left and right hemispheres can, in a limited sense, be thus traced back to the differences between olfaction and gustation. Smell is the original sense-modality in animals for acquiring information about targets that are at a distance and that would require approach toward them to be executed. Taste is the original sense for confirming that the thing one has approached and embraced is indeed pleasant and so to be swallowed, or unpleasant and so to be spit out. This observation should be credited to T. J. Crow, English neuroscientist.

In the history of the development of species in the animal kingdom, we see this twofold way of encountering reality present throughout. We see it beginning to be laterally specialized in mammals, higher mammals, and human beings. One of the ways concerns itself with things that are at a distance and that serve to summon the organism. The other way is concerned with things close at hand, which constitute either immediate pain or pleasure to the organism. This difference can also be illustrated, somewhat more interestingly perhaps, by the behavior of any human baby. A baby exhibits the same two synergisms of behavior that I have just described. One is that, if someone makes a loud noise, puts vinegar on his lips, or otherwise does something unpleasant to him, he will make both of his arms go up in the air, make both of his legs charge up and down, and scream loudly. If, instead of this global experience of unpleasantness, one provides him with a focal stimulus—an apple, a ball, one's face—his behavior is entirely different. Even at the very youngest age, this baby executes a very complex constellation of behaviors that include the following: first, he turns toward the object; second, he reaches out toward it; third, and most important, he emits a soft and pleasant vocalization. That behavior is executed by human babies four times more often with the right hand than with the left. Those who do execute it with the left hand tend to grow up to be left-handed. It appears that it is the left hemisphere, the soon-to-be-verbal hemisphere, that already programs this complex approach response. This example of the baby reveals the essential cognitive style of the left hemisphere: approach, anticipation, discrete and pleasant vocalization, and emotions and cognitions associated with that particular sequence of behavior.

Is such an approach-anticipation behavior to be found in the Bible? Even a brief tour through Scripture reminds us that this goal-oriented approach, this anticipatory state of mind, is central to the biblical faith. E. A. Speiser, the author of the Anchor Bible Commentary on the Book of Genesis, has presented a similar point of view about the Old Testament in the most eloquent way. As he puts it, the story of Abraham contains the "genesis of the whole biblical experience." For almost any writer of the Old or New Testament, Abraham is essentially a prototype of the entire biblical experience. The experience of Abraham is the experience of catching some kind of distant signal that is enough to summon him away from family, friends, town, and possessions and to call him to a thousand-mile journey around the rim of the desert, living as a wandering pilgrim for the rest of his life. Remember that he was no young upstart: he was an old man before he caught this new vision. There is an implied rejection of the secular city in Abraham's pilgrimage, but it is not a rejection alone that moves him. It is the promise, the destiny, the goal, which says that what he is to begin will one day be "a blessing to all nations." As the New Testament author of Hebrews says, he was not only leaving an old city behind but seeking a new one yet unbuilt.

An equally memorable example of this fundamental Old Testament experience is the Exodus, in many other ways the determinative experience of the Old Testament. Here, too, the emphasis throughout is on a promised land, a goal toward which a community must strive. Israelites may be disqualified from the promise, and for rather interesting reasons. Apparently, they had lived in slavery so long that is was hard for them to quit thinking like slaves, so at one point God decreed that nobody over twenty (Numbers 14:29) could enter the promised land, as though being born in a sedentary culture disqualified one from having the innovative outlook that is required to get across the river and begin the pioneering task of building a new nation.

If the Old Testament is suffused with this kind of anticipatory-approach style of behaving and thinking, how much more is the New Testament similarly anticipatory in its essence? We have only to remember how Jesus is always on the road, how much is made of the fact that he never gets where he is going, or that, when he finally does get to Jerusalem, he dies outside its gates. In describing his own individual religious style, Paul tells us that he once was a Hebrew of the Hebrews, circumcised on the eighth day, in all things law-abiding, decent, upright, honorable, and respectful, but that he gave it all up, he says, for Christ. Consider what he says in Philippians, chapter 3: "I put it all behind me, giving it all up, counting it all as worthless, so that I could stride on toward Christ." Then he goes on to say, "Not as though I had made him my own." Paul never said, "Jesus Christ belongs to me," as we sometimes say. He says instead, "I belong to him, and I am headed his way, but I am not there yet—poised between that which no longer is and that which is yet to come." He strides on day by day so that he may die as Christ did, be raised as Christ was, and so ultimately, perhaps, come to completion and fulfillment. There is no fulfillment or completion yet.

The most poignant illustration of this anticipatory attitude that characterizes the New, as well as the Old Testament, is to be found in the Apocalypse of John. We might superficially expect to look at the Christian vision of the future and see finally a time when there is no more antici-pation—a time when we need not look forward to anything, because it will all be here. John's last picture opens with the statement, "The dwelling place of God at long last is with man." He is going to dwell with them, to be their God. They are going to be his people at last. There is a city whose streets, indeed, are paved with gold. But this is no city in the sky; rather, it is a heavenly city placed down in the world. The gates of this city remain open all day, and there is no night. Through the gates of this city may come all the kings of the world with their trade. The last picture of the Bible is of the city, which is the church, whose gates still are open to the world and through which the world still comes. Furthermore, there is in this city a tree, whose leaves are specifically for the healing of the nations. Even John, the author of the Apocalypse, cannot foresee a time beyond which healing does not have to be done. He does not foresee a time when there still is not a mission for God's people.

If one of the characteristics of the verbal hemisphere is that it is ori-ented toward approach, then I think we can confirm this first premise from the scriptural records. The faith of the Bible is uniquely oriented toward a style of life and living, a style of thinking and emoting, that is approach directed, goal directed, and going somewhere, not a style that thinks that it has gotten there or that is particularly enjoying anything at the moment.

Second, if the religion of the Bible is left-hemispheric in central ways it also will be, according to contemporary neuroscience, a style that is highly particularistic, avoiding generalities and universals. This conclusion is really a corollary of the first point, because any sustained approach toward a target external to the organism requires that the target be isolated as a separate, individual, particular thing. The approach sequence is mobilized toward it in such a way that the part looms larger while all other things flee into the periphery and finally are not attended to at all. In the psychological literature this style of approach is called field independence, and recent studies indicate that this is uniquely the quality of the left hemisphere.

Patients with damage to the left hemisphere have difficulty isolating a figure and segregating it from the background, and the thing that correlates with field independence is verbal ability, not spatial ability. The data make it clear in many other ways that particularization, feature isolation, and segregation are all processes of left-hemisphere function.

How would this feature characterize the faith of the Bible? As a minor point, consider what Paul said about speaking in tongues. His commentary in the fourteenth chapter of First Corinthians on this subject is rich with psychological insight. Recall that he was annoyed by the fact that the Co-rinthians were fond of speaking in tongues. He argued that such religious ecstasy is relatively unproductive. It is as though one had a musical instrument but could not tell the difference between the notes. If the trumpet is vague, if its notes are indistinct from each other, how will one know what the tune is? Only a person who was convinced that his faith depended on precision would speak this way. Otherwise, he would say that he loved to get lost in the sea of imprecision, ambiguity, nothingness, or everythingness. Not this orientation for the apostle Paul; distinctness was crucial for him.

The more obvious arguments involve larger themes. The whole Old Testament is about a single chosen people. Often this particularity is offensive to the modern mind. But offensive or not, enjoyable or not, it is essential to the cognitive style of God's people. It is impossible, in their view, that the whole world could be selected at once for this mission. It is necessary that some group be chosen to make the blessing available to the rest of the group. If such is the scandal of the Old Testament, then certainly the scandal of the New Testament is the ultimate particularity inherent in the doctrine of the Incarnation itself. Here the specificity is so scandalous, so distinct, as to claim that everything God has to say to the world, he has said in the person of this one individual, Jesus. There is no greater particularity, no more field independence, than this. It is the ultimate in particularized faith. Like it or not, such is the essence of the New Testament. Even more so than the cognitions and emotions of approach, the very theology and the whole self-understanding of the Old and New Testament is highly particularistic, focused, and narrowed onto the kind of isolated individualization that only the left hemisphere, the verbal hemisphere, sustains.

Now the third test of my thesis. If the religion of the Bible is verbal (and therefore approach-oriented and particularistic), then we necessarily expect that it is language-oriented and that is does something special with language memory. I hold, therefore, that the biblical experience favors a specific kind of left-hemispheric memory, mainly memory for stories that depict real-life episodes and events. I sketch here this distiction in contemporary cognitive neuropsychology. We have long been struggling with the problem of how best to characterize memory. A proposal that Marcel Kinsbourne and I made a decade ago has captured considerable general interest (though not universal approbation). We proposed that the distinction that was already apparent in the experimental psychology of memory also applies to the pathology of memory. This distinction is due originally to Endel Tulving: on the one hand, there is the memory for episodes, which depends on personal experiences; on the other hand, there is the memory for truths, principles, facts, rules, and relationships. The first entails the memory of what one did this morning, some event of yesterday or of twenty years ago. It is located in time and place and by definition is unique. The second has to do with memory for the meanings of words, facts, rules, or relationships. This latter is called semantic memory precisely because it is the kind of memory that language itself represents. Some people lose the one, some lose the other, through brain damage; and yet the two ways of remembering are quite distinct and quite separate in the brain.

The kind of language that supports memory for episodes produces stories in which one tells what happened to oneself or to one's people at a certain time. The kind of language that supports semantic memory is propositional sentences of the form *A* equals *B:* "The grass is green". "God is . . . " (and one makes a list of his attributes). This latter kind of memory, supported by propositional sentences, appears not at all to be the kind of language that the Bible speaks. Instead, the Bible over and over again exhorts its readers to remember specific episodes of the past. Remarkably seldom does the Bible ask us to believe propositions, but surprisingly often it asks us to be sure that we do not forget the important events of individual and corporate religious history. It is as though the events and the memory of them are the critical data of religious experience.

This passion to remember events is familiar in the contemporary determination not to forget the Holocaust. Whenever one hears it talked about by the survivors, one always hears, "We must make sure that this is remembered for what is was." Only devotees of the faith of the Bible would think such remembrance is so important. Others more practical might say, "Why rub salt in the wounds? Can't we let bygones be bygones?" The Bible is never willing to forsake or abandon the past, and it collects its past as a memory storehouse of episodes. As the phrase over the gate at Dachau says, "Nie wieder" (never again). Dachau is preserved so that we will remember, lest we ever do it again. How else? Is this emphasis not central to the ritual of both the Old and New Testament?

At the Passover the question never fails—"Why is this night, of all nights, the one to remember?" Then the answer: "Because our fathers were delivered form their bondage in Egypt, we must not forget." The Christian echo to this is, as Paul put it, "I passed on to you . . . what was told and passed on to me, how the Lord on the night that he was betrayed took bread, broke it, and said, 'This is my body, do this in remembrance of me,' but likewise the cup after supping, saying, 'This is the cup of the new covenant.'" Here is the anticipatory note: "As often as you drink it, you remember the Lord's death until he returns." Again, the ritual of sacred memory puts the worshiper in the existential situation of looking both backward and forward but not sideways.

In summary, then, my thesis is that biblical faith uniquely draws upon the left hemisphere's anticipatory-approach mode, its emphasis on particularization, and its emphasis on narrative memory for events. I commend it against popular theories designed to confine religion to the ecstatic present.

A QUAKER'S VIEW
OF TRANSCENDENT EXPERIENCE

Douglas V. Steere

I grew up in the state of Michigan, and my religious experience as a boy was not untypical of many young Protestants. When I was fourteen, I was deeply moved by a young evangelist who gave me a sense of how God had singled me out and loved me. I joined the Methodist church, later transferred to the Presbyterian church to save a mile of walking each Sunday, and finally went to the Evangelical and Reformed chruch—not on any theological grounds but because they badly needed the help of my slide trombone in their Sunday school orchestra.

I studied agriculture at what was then Michigan Agricultural College, now Michigan State University, with potatoes as my specialty. At the end of the third year I found myself weary with activities, and my dearest friend and I decided to take a year off. At the age of nineteen, I taught chemistry and agriculture in a vigorous high school in Onaway in what might be classified as one of northern Michigan's least-developed counties. In addition to my teaching, I joined the county agricultural agent at night once or twice a week in journeys to remote parts of the county for meetings with farmers. The teaching and the work with the farmers went amazingly well, but as the year waned I had a deep inner sense of guidance that this work was not what I was put on earth for.

I returned to the college for my senior year, and in the course of it had the close friendship of a gifted member of the faculty. I never had a course with him, but on more than a few nights we talked far into the small hours. Although I had deep doubts about myself, he confirmed a feeling in me. I had worked my way through college, but with his encouragement I borrowed $1,000 and went to Harvard to study philosophy. In my college years the church had meant something to me. I suspect that my eagerness to read philosophy came from a longing to find, through it, a frame for the inner guidance that had so decisively drawn me away from the agricultural calling for which I was well trained. Instead of giving me this longed-for frame for my faith and experience, my study of philosophy wiped out what little faith I had. By spring of my first year at Harvard, I touched bottom and saw little to live for.

I remember that a Chinese student told me at that time of his own earlier conversion in his native city of Canton. Like most of his fellow students, he was lured to communism, but also felt a drawing toward the Christian way. He told me that early one morning he wakened suddenly and saw Jesus Christ standing beside his bed. Jesus had reached down and taken him by the hand and literally lifted him out of bed, and my friend knew instantly that he must renounce communism and follow Jesus. I felt wistful and wished that I could have such a decisive experience!

It was at this low point in the spring of 1924 that I met some fellow students to whom silent prayer and an inner sense of the guidance of God was very real. While I never joined their corporate group, several of them at the Episcopal Theological Seminary in Cambridge invited me to meet with them, and it was in these noonday sessions of silence that I began to pray again. By the end of this first Harvard year, I had been inwardly renewed in my faith. The renewal had come to me through silent prayer, into which I could bring anything. The sense of God's guidance grew in me as I tried to be faithful to what came during these seasons of prayer.

I describe in some detail here an incident that happened to me a year later. In the spring of my second year at Harvard, I decided to take the full battery of four comprehensive examinations that, if I passed, would clear the way for writing a doctoral thesis in philosophy. There was no compulsion to take these tests at this time. The previous autumn I had been awarded a Rhodes Scholarship for three years of study at Oxford, where I could go on in philosophy. Coming to Harvard with no undergraduate preparation in the field of philosophy, I had only a bare minimum of courses with which to tackle these examinations. But I had signed the papers to take them. The night before the ordeal of the first examination came, I had a crisis. I was deluged with all of the reasons for postponement. How much better to wait until I had two or three years of Oxford preparation! How stupid to risk the humiliation of failing if I took them now! I was sorely tempted to drop out the next morning, as a certain percentage of the candidates each year were reported to do.

That night at two o'clock, I knelt in prayer and asked for guidance. I stayed on my knees for half an hour, and the clear leading came to take the tests: to go into each one of the four with a quiet mind, to write what I could, and to accept without a quiver the outcome, whatever it might turn out to be. I went to bed with a quiet mind, slept soundly for four hours, and got up in the morning with an easy heart. I wrote the four three-hour papers in the next days with a steadiness and an ease that never deserted me. Some weeks later I was notified that I had passed the comprehensives and that I needed only an acceptable thesis and the language tests in order to fulfill the requirements for the doctorate.

It was in England that I first discovered to my surprise that there was something known as Quakerism that was centered in the guidance of the inward Christ and that was not simply a chapter in seventeenth-century history but was actively alive today. I had strained my back in rowing at Oriel College and was directed to Henry Gillett, a well-known Oxford doctor. He turned out to be a Quaker, and we struck up a friendship that went on through the rest of my time at Oxford and beyond. With a reading party of other Oxford students, I attended an hour's silent Quaker meeting at Old Jordan's Meeting House, where I first came to feel the power of Christ's indwelling spirit sweep through me and came to experience what the Quakers call a gathered or a covered meeting. Through Dr. Gillett I was invited to spend the night with Rufus Jones at Haverford College when I was on my way back to England for my third year at Oxford. From this visit I was invited to join Rufus Jones a year later as his junior colleague and to teach philosophy at Haverford College, for what turned out to be the rest of my professional life.

With this growing hunger to understand better the inner experience of divine guidance that had come to me, I decided in this final year (1927-1928) at Oxford to bury myself in Baron von Hügel's writing and to prepare myself to write a doctoral thesis for Harvard on his thought. I was quite free to move about, and in the course of that year I came to know a number of von Hügel's closest friends (he had died only in 1925). Professor Percy Gardiner, his literary executor, generously gave me access to von Hügel's unpublished papers.

In the course of these visits I came to know Evelyn Underhill (Mrs. Stuart Moore), who, for the last three years of von Hügel's life, had been under his spiritual direction. He was a Roman Catholic, but she was and remained an Anglican. He had immeasurably deepened her life, and in the next decade her books were treasures that I specially prized. In her earlier books on mysticism she had some plain words concerning the universality of the contemplative and the mystical dimension in the breast of every person. There she says, "Ordinary contemplation is open to all men; without it they are not wholly conscious or alive."[1] Without any radical discontinuity, she connects this ordinary contemplation with the highest glimpses the great mystics report of the ultimate togetherness when she says, "The spring of the amazing energy which enables the great mystic to rise to freedom and dominate his world is extant in all of us, an integral part of our humanity."[2]

On a visit I made to her home in London, I asked her if she herself had experienced the inward wave of love that had been witnessed to by many of the classic figures among the mystics that she wrote about. She was a slight figure of a woman, with sparkling eyes, and her reply to me was honest and direct. Looking directly at me, she said no, she had not had the major experiences that marked the great mystics, but she *had* experienced what it was to have "a slowing down." This and no more was her answer. In the closing fifteen years of her life that followed von Hügel's death, she gave much-sought-after retreats in an ancient retreat house at Pleshey in Essex. Her addresses there contained the seed kernels of the books that appeared one after another in those productive closing years of her life. These books and her letters, the latter posthumously published, are among the treasures that we have to draw upon to help us understand better the guiding power of God working within our lives.

I came to Haverford College in 1928, not as one transformed by a Damascus Road or an Aldersgate experience, but rather as one who knew something about what a contemporary Quaker, Elizabeth Vining, calls minor ecstasies. I had begun a journey and was still on the way. I do not count myself among the "once-born" or the "twice-born"; rather, my life has been an experience of continous conversion, and I found Haverford College a congenial atmosphere for continuing this journey. I persuaded Rufus Jones in my first semester at Haverford to give a small seminar on Meister Eckhart, who was a great passion of his. The half dozen of us who were in it, including Howard Thurman, found ourselves searched to the core by Eckhart's depiction of the transforming power of the Christ within.

The next year Dorothy Steere joined me at Haverford, and although not at that time members of the Society of Friends, we were included in a little group of Quakers who in 1930 established Pendle Hill, a small center

---

[1]Evelyn Underhill, *Practical Mysticism* (New York: E. F. Hutton, 1915) 11.

[2]Evelyn Underhill, *Mysticism* (London: Methuen, 1911) 532.

for study and contemplation that was located some ten miles from Haverford. Dr. Henry Hodgkin, a British Quaker medical doctor and religious statesman, who had spent twenty-five years in China, responded to our call to become the first director of Pendle Hill. I found him the greatest Christian I had ever come to know intimately. Few people knew the hidden roots of Henry Hodgkin's spiritual life. Early each morning he spent at least an hour that was divided between his silent time of inward listening in prayer, his reading in some devotional classic, and his pouring out in a secret day-book the insights and concerns that had come to him. He spoke often of "the inward tendering." At the end of the two swift years, he was fatally stricken with cancer. But in these two critical years he launched Pendle Hill, a precious island of spiritual and social guidance that has touched the lives of many people in the past half century of its existence.

Although Dorothy and I were not members of the Society of Friends, we were both deeply moved by the corporate meetings on the basis of silence and found that, in the climate of this group, the interior presence of Christ moved within us and centered and renewed our dispersed lives and, from time to time, laid on us things to be done. In 1930, we were invited to join with half a dozen others in opening a beautiful old meetinghouse located in the country, some four miles from Haverford. It had been built in 1718 but had been closed in about 1880, as its members had nearly all moved away. Now with motor cars more common, Radnor Meeting became accessible again. This small cluster of Christians gathered each Sunday morning in a room where the heating was supplied by an old pot-bellied stove, and the lighting, by candles and oil lamps.

In these same years I was drawn into the work of the American Friends Service Committee. At this time we were especially concerned for the coalfields of Western Pennsylvania and of West Virginia, where, because of the Depression and closing of the mines, people were literally starving. Local, county, and state funds were exhausted, and no federal aid was in existence. We were feeding children in that whole area, and in order to give some Christmas leave to our regular team of workers there, I took a small group of Quaker students into Logan, West Virginia, to carry on this feeding over the holidays. I saw what it meant for unemployed miners and their families to live on the proceeds of picking over garbage dumps and of greens gathered from the woods.

During these first four years at Haverford, Dorothy and I were reluctant to join the Quakers. Neither of us was a "joiner" in our adulthood, and now that we expected a child and faced mounting duties, we continued to hold back. In the spring of 1932, we read John Woolman's *Journal*. Woolman was a Quaker from Mt. Holly, New Jersey, who lived from 1720 to 1772 and who, from his mid-twenties until his death, found the concern and the time to convince the Society of Friends to desist from owning slaves. In this moving *Journal* we found that our last hesitations about joining the Society of Friends had quietly melted away. For in Woolman, we discovered someone who lived in the world as we did. He was married and had a family as we did; he supported his family and his journeys by his own labor as we meant to do. In Woolman we found a person in whom the inward tendering and the concern for his fellows that the Guide had laid upon him were brought together and carried out. We both agreed that, with all our frailties, the time had come for us to throw in our lot with the Quakers. We applied for membership and were admitted.

Looking back at our life in the 1960s—which saw us develop close relationships with the Roman Catholics, attend three sessions of the Vatican Council II, and, with Father Godfrey Dickman, found the Ecumenical Institute for Spirituality—we can see how the Inward Guide often prepares us far in advance for the work that will be laid upon us later. In 1931, Dr. Maria Schluter-Hermkes, a distinguished Roman Catholic scholar, was brought to this country by the Carl Schurz Foundation to lecture on several of the great Roman Catholic saints. I met her, and we found much common ground. Since I knew German, she encouraged me to come to Germany on my first sabbatical leave from Haverford; she promised that she and her husband would open to me the world of German Roman Catholic spirituality.

Haverford College generously gave me this leave in 1933-1934, and with arrangements made for Dorothy to join me in midyear, I crossed to Germany in August 1933, the first Hitler year. Through the husband of Dr. Schulter-Hermkes, I was invited to spend a month in the great Benedictine monastery of Maria Laach, well above the Rhine in the Andernach area. In due time I was taken to meet the famous Abbot Herwegen. With pleasant chuckles, he chided me a little for coming to a Benedictine monastery for a month of personal retreats and private piety. For them, salvation came rather from being part of a family or a community and not by any private nurturing! Nevertheless he sent me a companion and spiritual guide, Father Damasus Winzen, a young monk of almost exactly my own age.

At the time I did not realize that Damasus Winzen was to become one of the most beloved friends of my life. He suggested that we read and discuss together *Agape and Eros,* written by the Lutheran professor Nygren and only recently translated from the Swedish. The book's overwhelming accent on the undeserved grace and love that God pours out on us searched me deeply during those days. One afternoon when I was out walking, I saw a peasant farmer with a great sling of wheat tied over his left shoulder.

Reaching his right hand deep into this sling, I saw him fling out the seed-wheat recklessly onto the harrowed land as he moved across the field. There was no skimping, no measuring, no looking back, but only the wanton forward thrusting of his gait as he marched across the field. I was overwhelmed with its likeness to God's grace. In the same moment I was swept with an overpowering wave of love for my mother, who through all these years had poured out on me that very kind of caring. Our family had never been very demonstrative, and we were not given to express our affections very openly. But now I turned my steps back to the monastery, and going to my room, I wrote my mother a love letter in which I cast aside all barriers and told her how much I loved her and how suddenly I had come to realize how little I had thanked her or shown what that love of hers had meant to me. Something broke in me at this point; I began to see and feel that, at the bottom of it all, it is love that matters, love that opens the way, and that Augustine is right when he says that "We come to God by love and not by navigation" (that is, by detailed spiritual charts). Now I could understand in a new way what the old nineteenth-century Scot, George MacDonald, meant when he wrote, "Pray to the God of sparrows, rabbits and men, who never leaves anyone out of his ken."

Strangely enough, Father Damasus came to the United States two years later on a commission to see where Maria Laach might be lodged in this country, should the Nazi persecution drive the Benedictines out of Germany. This never occurred, but Father Damasus stayed on here for the rest of his life, and our friendship kept deepening with the years. In 1951, he founded a vigorous new monastery called Mt. Saviour, which lies between Elmira and Corning in the state of New York. Forty men had joined it before he slipped away in 1971. Only a few months before his death, Father Damasus expressed with power and clarity the very heart of my own experience of that peasant farmer almost forty years before. He told a companion, "When I look back upon the seventy years of my own life, I see quite clearly that I owe my present inner happiness, my peace, my confidence and my joy essentially to one fact: I am certain that I am infinitely loved by God."

My scholarly friend Maria Schluter-Hermkes more than fulfilled her promise to open the way for me to come to know some of the great German spirits in the Roman Catholic community. I was able to meet Alois Dempf, Theodore Haecker, Dr. Schöningh (the editor of *Hochland*, the finest Catholic journal in the country), and the Eckhart scholar Joseph Bernhart. When I got to Berlin I was able not only to meet Romano Guardini, who, in the German Catholic world, scarcely had an equal in mind or spirit in that period, but also to have evenings with him in his home at Eichkampf.

In the autumn and spring of 1936-1937, I found an old lady who lived in Solebury, Pennsylvania, an hour's journey from Haverford, who took me in and gave me board and room weekends and let me have the use of a folding table in her ancient woodshed. There I wrote my book, *Prayer and Worship,* for the Hazen series. Twenty-five years later I enlarged upon it at the Methodists' urging. Under the title *Dimensions of Prayer,* it became their study book for the year 1962. In this second book on prayer, I especially accented the importance of the way that I enter prayer. I am sympathetic with the use of any meditation practices that can still the mind and relax the body, but they are vestibule exercises. When I am ready to enter prayer, I feel it wise not to enter it in a state of mind where I project the prayer, where I take the initiative in cranking it up. Instead, it makes such a difference if I enter it in awesome awareness that I am besieged by and immersed in a love that is utterly without qualification. It is not that God loves me *if,* but simply that God loves me! Von Hügel's word is that "it is God who wakes and God who slakes our thirst."

Meister Eckhart in one of his eloquent sermons gives his own witness to this operation of the divine initiative: "God is foolishly in love with me. He seems to have forgotten heaven and earth and deity; his entire business is with me alone, to give me everything to comfort me. He gives it to me suddenly; He gives it to me wholly; He gives it to me perfectly; He gives it to me all the time; and He gives it to all creatures." Eckhart pauses, and then he asks, "Why are you not aware of it?" And he answers his own question: "Because you are not at home in the soul's inmost center."[3]

Bernard of Clairvaux, in the twelfth century, had a lovely passage in one of his sermons to his monks in which he deals with eager brothers who try to creep into the chapel before the Cistercian company's appointed hour of morning gathering at 3:15 A.M., hoping perhaps that they might sometime manage to get into their place before God came! "Do you awake?" Bernard asks; "Well He, too, is awake; if you rise in the nightime, if you anticipate to your utmost your earliest awaking, you will find Him waking. You will never anticipate His awakeness. In such an intercourse, you will always be rash if you attribute any priority or predominant share to yourself. For He loves both more than you and before you love at all."[4]

It is hard for me to underline sufficiently what a difference it makes to enter prayer with a deep consciousness of this divine initiative. To be con-

---

[3]*Meister Echkart,* ed. F. Pfeifer, trans. C. de B. Evans (London: Watkins, 1924) 295.

[4]*St. Bernard on Song of Songs* (London: Mowbray, 1952).

scious that, long before I make my response in prayer at all, something immensely costly and penetrating has been going on; that it continues during my prayer; and that it continues to undergird my very life when I have turned from conscious acts of prayer to my other tasks of the day. This awareness, and nothing short of it, gives to prayer its true setting. "Prayer is a response to God's Isness" is another way to put it. My prayer did not begin this encompassing love. That love has been like a poultice laid over me and laid over the world for its healing long before I came on the scene. When I pray I simply enter into this ongoing stream, and my act of prayer, precious and important as it truly is, is swept up into something infinitely vast and is cleansed for use.

I will not attempt here to go beyond naming the familiar sequence of praying that is stirred by this realization of God's initiative. There are the stages of adoration and thankfulness, contrition and yielding, petition and intercession, and finally, listening for the biddings that are often laid upon us by the Inward Guide for taking part in the interpersonal life of our time. Yet, all of these voluntary aspects of my prayer are greatly affected by the door through which they enter. Paul Claudel, the French poet, says that "all prayer is simply thankfulness that God is!"

My own life in these years was being blessed by the weekly hour of corporate prayer in the steadily growing little Radnor Meeting. I must say something about this experience, else I cannot explain the Quaker notion of the guiding hand of God in our lives that the meeting renews in us or explore the holy nudges and concerns that are laid on us for service far beyond the meeting doors.

Alexander Parker, a trusted friend of George Fox, has a brief word of advice for the conduct of such a corporate meeting for worship:

> The first that enters into the place of your meeting, be not careless nor wander up and down either in body or mind, but innocently sit down in some place and turn in thy mind to the Light, and wait upon God simply as if none were present but the Lord, and here thou art strong. When the next come in, let them in simplicity of heart sit down and turn to the same Light, and wait in the Spirit, and so all the rest coming in the fear of the Lord, sit down in pure stillness and silence of all flesh, and wait in the Light. A few that are thus gathered by the arm of the Lord into the unity of the spirit, this is a sweet and precious meeting in which all are met in the Lord.[5]

There are two stories about strangers getting into such a silent meeting by mistake and sitting for an hour in bewildered expectancy of hearing a sermon. The first tells of one of these visitors turning to his companion and saying at the close of the hour when all rose to leave, "Doesn't this beat

---

[5]Alexander Parker, *Letters to Friends,* ed. A. R. Barclay (1841) 365-66.

the devil." An old Quaker who overheard the remark leaned over to him and said, "Friend, that is exactly what this meeting is for." Another bewildered visitor asked a Quaker at the close of the meeting, "When does the service begin?" only to receive the prompt reply, "Now."

I should add that there is always complete liberty on the part of either men or women to share briefly any message that might be given to them for the meeting, although it is not uncommon for the hour to pass in complete silence. After some years of experience in these corporate meetings for worship, I was once asked to write down what the meeting for worship meant to me. I include here two paragraphs from my response to this request.

> The meeting for worship has sent tears down my cheeks. It has given me specific things to be done and the strength to undertake them. It has, on a few occasions, laid on my heart rimless concerns whose precise structure and whose outcome I could not foresee and kept them before me until they came to some degree of clarity. It has called me into the intercessory chain-gang to pray for other people and for situations where the need was urgent. It has changed my mind when I did not mean to change it. It has firmed me up when I might have yielded. It has rested me. It has upset my sluggish rest. It has helped prepare me to live. It has fortified me in knowing that my ashes will eventually lie in the earth only a couple of hundred feet from where I am sitting at Radnor Meeting and has helped me to feel the presence of the One who can bear me now and bear me then.
>
> It has scarified me and broken down the hull of my life and shown me how I might live. It has warned me that I am too cowardly to live that way, but reminded me for good measure that it is not what I give that makes me suffer but what I hold back! It has comforted and quieted me when I was torn and hurt, and it has dug up the garden of my soul when I thought the present produce was all I could manage. In it I have physically slept and again I have been terribly awake. In it my mind has wandered like a hummingbird on holiday and yet in it I have felt moments of intensity and of concentration and awareness that have shown me what life could be like.

In a far more cultivated fashion, Donald Court, a highly esteemed British Quaker doctor and professor of public medicine at the University of Leeds, speaks of both the daily times of stillness and the weekly corporate meeting for worship. Of them he says, "These are the times to reach down to a level where I can see myself and my work straight, where that strength we call love can break through my anxiety and teach me how to respond instead of to react . . . how to open the road to a spirit blocked by busyness, self-importance, self-indulgence, self-pity, depression and despair. I could not have coped, perhaps even survived, the last 35 years without the meeting for worship."[6] In Donald Court's exposure of the healing return to wholeness that has come to him in the corporate silent meeting, he is describing the gathering power of the Inward Christ.

---

[6]Donald Court, *The Friend*, vol. 128, no. 38 (1970): 1109.

In these nurturing seasons of corporate waiting in the meeting for worship, from time to time we seem to be taken beyond ourselves, and instead of *praying,* we seem to be prayed *in.* Friends call such an occasion a gathered or a covered meeting. An old Russian Orthodox saint of the ancient past was speaking about such a moment in private prayer in the following admonition: "When the Holy Spirit speaks, *stop* praying!"

I want to share with you a scene from a little book called *Beginning to Pray,* written by the Russian Orthodox Archbishop of London, Anthony Bloom. He describes these moments when effortful prayer is meant to stop and where the gift of the effortless sense of the Presence appears:

About twenty years ago soon after my ordination, I was sent before Christmas to an old people's home. There lived an old lady who came to see me after my first celebration and said, "Father, I would like to have advice about prayer." So I said, "O yes, ask so and so." She said, "All these years I have been asking people who are reputed to know about prayers and they have never given me a sensible reply, so I thought that as you probably know nothing, you might possibly blunder out the right thing." That was a very encouraging situation! And so I said, "What is your problem?" The old lady said, "These fourteen years I have been praying the Jesus Prayer almost continually, and never have I perceived God's presence at all." I said, "If you speak all the time, you don't give God a chance to place a word in." She said, "What shall I do?" "Go to your room after breakfast and put it right . . . light your little lamp before the ikon that you have and first of all take stock of your room. Just sit, look round, and try to see where you live, because I am sure that if you have prayed all these fourteen years it is a long time since you have seen your room. And then take your knitting and for fifteen minutes knit before the face of God, but I forbid you to say one word of prayer. You just knit and try to enjoy the peace of your room."

She didn't think it was very pious advice but she took it. After awhile she came to see me and said, "You know, it works." I said, "What works, what happens?" because I was very curious to know how my advice worked. And she said, "I did just what you advised me to do. I got up, washed, put my room right, had breakfast, came back, made sure that nothing was there that would worry me, and then I settled in my armchair and thought, 'Oh how nice, I have fifteen minutes during which I can do nothing without being guilty!' and I looked round and for the first time in years I thought, 'Goodness what a nice room I live in. . . . ' " Then she said, "I felt so quiet because the room was so peaceful. There was a clock ticking but it didn't disturb the silence, its ticking just underlined the fact that everything was so still and after a while I remembered that I must knit before the face of God, and so I began to knit. And I became more and more aware of the silence. The needles hit the armrest of my chair, the clock was ticking peacefully, there was nothing to bother about, I had no need of straining myself, and then I perceived that this silence was not simply an absence of something but a presence of something. The silence had a density, a richness, and it began to pervade me. . . . The silence around began to come and meet the silence in me. . . . All of a sudden I perceived that the silence was a Presence. At the heart of the silence there was Him who is all stillness, all peace, all poise." [7]

---

[7] Anthony Bloom, *Beginning to Pray* (New York: Paulist) 59-61.

In his *Varieties of Religious Experience,* William James writes, "Our normal working consciousness, rational consciousness we call it, is but one special type of consciousness while all about it, parted from it by the filament of screens, there lie potential forms of consciousness entirely different. We may go through life without suspecting their existence, but supply the requisite stimulus and at a touch, they are there."[8] William Blake says, "If the doors of perception were cleansed, everything would appear to man as it is, infinite."

Whether it is on another level of consciousness or whether the doors of perception are secretly cleansed, in these moments of a gathered meeting the Quaker experience is that, with this gift of the Presence and with its accompanying sense of deepened solidarity with our fellow creatures, there seem to come, now to this person and now to that, the holy nudges, the tasks, the concerns that need to be undertaken. These concerns can and do, of course, come in any situation, but the corporate meeting for worship has been found to be of special importance in initiating and dealing with them. These seeds of concerns are not put there on an ornamental basis. They are secretly given to us to be worked over and to be acted upon. The price of the neglect or the refusal of such leadings may not be small.

Archbishop William Temple, in his great Gifford Lectures *Nature, Man, and God,* suggests that the eternal nature of God is unchanging but that this strategy is infinitely variable. The implication of this suggestion is that if, when a task is laid on me from within, I shun it or neglect it, the whole strategy may have to be changed! Temple suggests, in other words, that my response to the holy nudge may have cosmic consequences!

The corporate meeting for worship is often spoken of as being held on the basis of silence and obedience. Thomas Mann, in an address at the Library of Congress, once confided, "Were I to determine what I personally mean by religiousness, I should say it is attentiveness and obedience." Without attentiveness in both private and public worship, there can be only a confirmation of the African proverb that says, "When God speaks, he does not wake up the sleeper." Unless this precious attentiveness is linked to obedience, however, the deeper bond is missing. To come near to God is to change, and unless there is obedience—a change of will and a willingness to open the sealed orders and seek to carry them out—I have failed the Love that bid me to join him.

Romano Guardini first urged me to read the books of a contemporary Swiss medical doctor and Christian mystic who wrote under the name of Adrienne von Speyr. In one of her books, called *The Word,* she says,

---

[8]William James, *Varieties of Religious Experience* (New York: Longmans) 388.

To receive God means to make room for God, whatever he may be or bring. It may be only a call to be prepared, a vague indefinite and undefinable demand, or on the other hand, it may be a visible or intelligible task; it may be a single action, or just one word spoken. . . . Once open to the Light man may ask God to claim him more essentially and more profoundly. But on one condition only, on condition that he does not refuse the first small act that God demands of him.[9]

She might well have gone on to add that this condition applies not only to the "first small act" but to the countless others that are to follow.

Three strong voices from the seventeeth-century underline the Guide's laying on us specific things to be done as well as the promptness required in carrying out these inward directions. Francis de Sales goes as far as to define devotion in terms of the swiftness with which we respond to the inner bidding: "Devotion is the promptitude, fervor, affection and agility which we show in service of God." He extends this insight: "God requires a faithful fulfillment of the merest trifle given to us to do, rather than the most ardent aspiration to things to which we are not called." In Britain a few decades later, the beloved seventeenth-century Quaker, Isaac Pennington, wrote a line in a letter that I have always treasured. In it he says, "There is that near you which will guide you. O wait for it and be sure that ye keep to it." Augustine Baker, the seventeenth-century Benedictine who wrote the classic *Holy Wisdom,* put it all in seven words, "Mind your call; that's all in all."

This dimension of obedience—this "mind your call" and the following of the Guide—is such a vital part of the Quaker religious experience that I am going to cite briefly two classic examples and then conclude with some personal witness to this obedience dimension, together with the visible and invisible barriers that confront it. Neurius Mendenhall was a Quaker who with his family headed the New Garden Friends Boarding School in Greensboro, North Carolina, in the years that led up to the Civil War. As the inevitability of the Civil War became more apparent and as it became clear that North Carolina was squarely united with the Confederate cause of breaking with the Union and keeping the institution of slavery, of which the Mendenhall family disapproved, they had finally come to the decision that, like so many Quakers in that region, they should promptly emigrate to Ohio or Indiana in the North. This action, however, meant abandoning the New Garden Friends Boarding School. But the die was cast, and the family, with all of their transportable belongings, was at the train station in Greensboro ready to leave.

---

[9]Adrienne von Speyr, *The Word,* trans. Alexander Dru (London: Collins, 1955) 9.

In spite of the many complications of reopening the decision to leave that had been so burningly clear to them up to this time, the Inward Guide laid firmly on Neurius Mendenhall that he must not leave, that he must return to the school, and that come what would, he must bear his witness right there where he had been placed. He shared this call with his wife and she concurred. They carted their goods and their family back to their home and settled in. He kept the school open all during the Civil War and took a leading role in the Reconstruction period that followed those horrible years. Today New Garden Friends Boarding School is Guilford College, one of the most promising smaller colleges in the South.

Emma Noble was the wife of a foreman in a locomotive works near Oxford in Britain. In the early 1920s, the unemployment and misery in the coal-mining areas of South Wales were appalling. It came to her in a Quaker meeting for worship that she should visit this area and see if there was anything that the Quakers could do in this region to lessen the pain. Her husband agreed, and a small "committee of clearness" in the meeting found the concern in right ordering and encouraged her to follow it. In the first valley that she visited in South Wales, there seemed to be no opening for the kind of assistance that the Friends could offer. She did not feel released to return home, however, and extending her journey, she looked into the Rhonda Valley. In the course of some days there, a way began to open, and the real purpose of her journey began to emerge. Out of the visit a way was found to release the Nobles for what turned out to be many years of service, and a longtime program of work unfolded that eventually involved university people, members of parliament, a royal visit, and finally a program of legislation to help ease the ugly situation. Her first small step, which was in part a mistaken one, led to further steps and ultimately to a deeper and deeper involvement.

These examples give at least a glimpse of the manner in which concerns arise and are carried out, with failures and unpredictable breakthroughs all mixed together. Malty Babcock, a British religious leader in the last generation, used to say that Jesus promised those who would follow his leadings only three things: that they should be absurdly happy, entirely fearless, and always in trouble! Most concerns begin as seeds that may need scarifying in order to grow. Not only is the seed of concern something that needs careful treatment to unfold, but the one to whom the concern has come may often enough be quite unready to carry it out until he or she has been changed and reshaped in ways that call for great flexibility and openness. Even the members of the community that is to encourage and support the concern may have to go through painful change before they are ready to unite with it.

These leadings of the Guide come to us via our own psychological mechanisms and are capable therefore of blemish. A seasoned Friend has a certain debonair attitude about being made a fool of and has learned to wait and to see how the concern, and his motives for that concern, looks the next day or the next week. He knows enough to allow his own private detective agency to examine all aspects of his concern. He sees how it looks after wise and trusted people whom he has consulted have given their opinion of it. If the concern can endure this kind of scrutiny, he may take it to a committee of clearness that he may select himself, or if it involves the meeting, he may ask to bring it to a monthly meeting for business. The "when in doubt, wait" motto, though often painful in its implications for the person or persons involved, has often been found to test the flexibility and centeredness of the bearer of the concern. If this embarrassing waiting, or the prospect of it, succeeds in dissolving away the concern, its rootlessness has been exposed, and it withers away and is buried. Albert Schweitzer once suggested that, when some compassionate venture, perhaps of an innovative sort, is proposed, we must not expect people to clear stones from our path. Rather, they may roll a few extra boulders onto it just to see if we really mean it!

My own life as a professor of philosophy has, from the time I was thirty-six years of age, been sprinkled with interwoven concerns for situations in the world; and through Haverford College's academic generosity, I have been able to travel under these concerns in Europe and, later with my wife in Africa and Asia, on many missions for the American Friends Service Committee. I have known the delay, the blockings, and the yielding; often the concern has turned out to be very different from what I had originally conceived it to be. I have also experienced breakthroughs that went beyond my fondest hopes. I had been in Finland in 1927 and was deeply drawn to its fascinating people. The frightful winter war with Russia in 1939-1940 had taken a terrible toll, and when I was called upon by the committee to spend some months in Germany in the last half of 1940, I felt a strong leading to visit Finland and to see if anything could be done to ease their sense of despair and of being totally abandoned. Over the months I was repeatedly refused the necessary German exit and reentry visas, in spite of vigorous efforts to help me from what remained of the Christian underground at that time. Finally at the end of November, when my time in Germany was almost up, I was informed by the ministry that had assisted me in these requests that the final denial, the "Nicht gestattet," had come from the Gestapo at Alexander Platz and that the matter was closed.

This concern of mine had been from the depths, and I went back quite shaken to the little Berlin Quaker Center and settled in the meetinghouse room for a time of quiet. In the course of the silent waiting, it seemed right that I should go to Dr. Diekoff, the German ambassador to the United States, who sat in Berlin during the war period, and should describe my situation, and then that I should lay aside this concern, for all its gripping character, and give myself fully to another round of visits to the German Quakers before leaving for America at the end of the year.

I set out the next day on this round of visits. Three days later, when I was visiting a brave Christian pastor who lived near Buckeburg and who was very close to the Society of Friends, I was called back to Berlin by my colleagues there. He had just been notified by the Gestapo in Berlin that my exit and reentry visas were waiting for me at Alexander Platz! I was able, with his help, to fly to Sweden the next evening and to make the Finnish visit, a visit that in many ways led to the Quaker relief work for the north of Finland that I was to organize five years later. An International Folk-Highschool called Viittakivi also grew out of the relief work, as did the work camp that was carried on in cooperation with the Finnish Christian Settlement Movement. This experience of being willing to accept the refusal of my journey to Finland, followed by its restoration, seemed to me almost as if intended to teach me the meaning of the searching counsel of Berulle, the old seventeenth-century spiritual guide: "To go or to stay is the same"; only as I was willing to give it up and to stay was the way open for me to go forward.

I will mention only one other situation as a personal example of a concern that failed completely yet one that emerged some years later in a dramatically different form and that in the end actually carried out the original leading in an amazing fashion. In 1960, on a mission for the American Friends Service Committee in India, my wife and I were much drawn to confer and to search for a suitable place for a modest Quaker ashram where Guirdal Malik, an Indian Quaker of deep spiritual gifts, would serve as a warden and spiritual presence. We thought of it as an ecumenical center of hospitality where, from time to time, spiritual personalities from the Christian and other great world religions would be invited to live together for a season and irradiate each other with the rich experiences of their different traditions. The search utterly failed.

In 1967, seven years later, my earlier leading to expose to each other Christians and Hindus in India, and Christians and Zen Buddhists in Japan, surfaced yet again. With the approval of the Friends World Committee and a year of careful preparation (where I was admirably assisted by several Roman Catholic colleagues whom I had known at Vatican II in Rome), two residential colloquia, one of five days and the other of seven, were able to be held, one in Japan and one in India. Each colloquium was made up of ten most carefully chosen Christian men of the spirit, who in Japan were matched by ten Zen Buddhist masters and in India by ten outstanding Hindu sadhus and scholars. In each case they were the guests of the Quakers, but the meetings were held not·on Quaker soil or under a Quaker roof, for which I had been searching fruitlessly in 1960, but in most suitable conference centers in each country!

In August 1983, this Japanese colloquium held its seventeenth annual meeting for three days in Kyoto, having alternated every other year with a meeting in Tokyo. A moving book appeared in 1977 called *A Zen-Christian Pilgrimage*. It contained twenty-six personal testimonies of participants who described what this experience of meeting annually for a whole decade with those of another religion had meant to their own religious lives. Four years later the English translation of the book was printed. Guirdal Malik is no longer alive, and there is still no physically established Quaker ashram in either country! Yet as in the unforeseen unfolding of so many concerns, the waiting, the drastic reshaping, or even the deferment to a future generation does not invalidate the significance of their work.

On a bulletin board in the little Quaker meetinghouse in Australia's Adelaide, I once saw some words from a British Quaker educator, the late Harold Loucks, that read, "An act of love that fails is just as much a part of the divine life as an act of love that succeeds. For love is measured by its fullness and not by its reception." To do what we are led to do by concern and to leave the rest with the Master Harvester seems to Quakers to be the way indicated.

When, late in his life, John Woolman felt drawn to make a dangerous trip to Wehaloosing in order to visit a friendly tribe of Indians who had called on the Quakers in Philadelphia, he wrote in his *Journal*, "Love was the first motion." In this chapter I have been witnessing to my faith and experience that Love *is* the first motion, a Love that will not let us go, yet a Love that lures us to respond and to follow the biddings of the Inward Guide.

To understand the Christian religion, with all of its widely varying forms of worship and expression—its mystical, its prophetic, its mutual-caring outreach to the world's needs—one must return to the Love at the heart of things that undergirds us all and that is above all to realize that we are not in life alone. Arthur Gossip, a hard-bitten pastor in a slum church in Glasgow, tells of how, at the end of a long day of visiting his parishioners, he arrived late in the afternoon at a five-story tenement where the last family on his list for that day lived at the very top. He was exhausted and said to himself, "It's too far up. I'll come tomorrow." He was about to turn away when a pair of stooped grey shoulders seemed to brush past him and start up the stairs with the word, "Then I'll have to go alone." Arthur Gossip added, "We went up together."

A CHRISTIAN WAY
TO TRANSFORMATION

M. Basil Pennington, O.C.S.O.

A shrinking global village with its increasingly mobile population often gifts us with very interesting and enriching neighbors. We have had such an experience at St. Joseph's Abbey. Among our neighbors today are a Hindu ashram and a Buddhist meditation center. Swami Satchidananda has established to the south of us a large, prosperous monastery that his disciples refer to as Yogaville East. To the north of us there is an Insight Meditation Center of the Thervada tradition. I am happy to say that relations with these brothers and sisters are the very best. We mutually share by invitation in each other's special festive celebrations. The Buddhist center especially has encouraged the Christians who come there for the purpose of learning meditation to visit the abbey for help in placing their new practice in the context of their Christian life.

Periodically, there are those who make the rounds. They go to the ashram and learn what they can of the eight limbs of Yoga. They spend some time at the meditation center learning insight meditation. And then they knock at our door and ask, What is your method?

My usual answer is that our whole life is our method. As the early Christians expressed it, we have entered into "the Way." Our Master and Lord, who spoke of himself as "the Way and the Truth and the Life," coming from the fullness of the Jewish tradition, summed up his way in the two great commandments: "The first and greatest commandment is this:

You shall love the Lord your God with your whole mind, your whole heart, your whole soul, and your whole strength. And the second is like unto this: You shall love your neighbor as yourself.'' He went on to modify the second, saying, ''I give you a new commandment: You shall love one another as I have loved you.'' Making it clear that ''greater love than this has no man than he lay down his life for his friends,'' he went on to do just that. He laid down his life for all of us, his friends.

The way of the Christian, then, is to love the Lord our God and one another, even to the point of laying down our lives for each other. Actual physical martyrdom may be the exception, though it is more common today than in any previous period of Christian history. But we are all called to take up our cross daily and follow our Master. ''Unless the grain of wheat fall into the ground and die, it remains itself alone. But if it dies, it will bear much fruit.''

This response, that our whole life is our method, usually does not satisfy the insistent inquirer. He or she has found among the Hindus and Buddhists a seemingly concise method or practice and is looking for the same among the Christians. At this point, insisting always that the practice must nurture a full pursuit of the Way and that, outside of such a context, it may well be fruitless, I tell our inquirer that our method is *lectio*.

''What is that?'' is the usual response to such a statement. I deliberately leave the word in Latin, for the simple translation, ''reading,'' certainly betrays the meaning. More important, *lectio* or *lectio divina* always connotes for the Christian coming out of our tradition a whole process summed up in the four words: *lectio, meditatio, oratio,* and *contemplatio.* This process is geared toward a transformation of consciousness and life. ''Let this mind be in you which was in Christ Jesus,'' says Paul. Our aim is to have the ''mind of Christ,'' to see and evaluate things, to respond to reality in the way Christ our Lord and Master does—to see things as God sees them, to share in the divine consciousness. I develop here this Christian way or process.

Lectio cannot simply mean ''reading,'' even though that is its literal translation. We are speaking of a way of Christian spirituality that prevailed through many centuries when the vast number of Christian people could not read. I think *lectio* here can most properly be understood as meaning ''to receive the revelation.'' It can be perceived immediately that this is a way most consonant with Christianity. We Christians, sharing this heritage in part with our Jewish brothers and sisters, are sons and daughters of the Book. God, who of old spoke first through the creation and then through the Prophets, has in these last days spoken to us through his incarnate Son, our Lord Jesus.

Lectio most properly resides in hearing the Word of God. We do this as a Christian people when we gather in our communal worship. The Reformers of the sixteenth century quite rightly laid great emphasis on this setting. The recent liturgical reforms in the Roman Catholic church have also emphasized it.

In an earlier period, memories seem to have been sharper or were used more. It was not uncommon for an average Christian to know by heart extensive passages of Scripture, perhaps even the whole of the Gospels and the Psalter. Men such as the venerable abbot Bernard of Clairvaux were reputed to know the whole Bible. These Christians, then, always carried the Scriptures with them and at any moment, drawing on memory, could hear the Word of God.

The Word of God revealed itself in other ways too—in the shared faith of sisters and brothers, for example. The Reformers laid great stress on the sermon, as did the Fathers, whose great sermons have come down to us. Faith is also shared in less formal settings, in small groups, or in a one-to-one encounter. Out of our experience of the Word, enlightened by the Holy Spirit, we speak the Word to one another.

The Word can be heard through other media—certainly through music. Powerful hymns repeat themselves insistently within us: "Amazing Grace, how sweet the sound." Art, the frescoes, icons, and stained-glass windows are also means by which the Word is spoken. The earliest Christian assemblies gathering in homes and catacombs adorned the walls of their meeting places with scenes from the Scriptures. Our Eastern Christian sisters and brothers find a real presence in the icons and enshrine them in their homes as well as in their churches. The whole of the Scriptures are depicted in the windows of the great medieval cathedrals, such as Chartres.

The Master Artist does not cease to reveal himself in his masterpiece, the creation. As Paul reminded the Romans, for the mind that would see, God has always been there to be seen. Bernard of Clairvaux is noted for the saying that has been rendered into rather trite English, "I have found God more in the trees and the brooks than in the books." Above all does God reveal himself in that which is greatest in all creation, his own image and likeness, the graced person. In others and in our very selves, we can experience the goodness and love of God, God himself, if we would but be still and know that he is God.

In colloquial English we have the expression "I read you." It implies that I fully understand what someone is trying to convey to me. To read in this sense is perhaps a good translation of *lectio*—to understand God and all he is saying, in all the many ways he is speaking.

Lectio, then, does not necessarily mean sitting with a book. It can mean looking at a work of art, standing before an icon, listening to a friend's word of faith, or taking a walk, letting the beauty of the creation that often lies beneath layers of sin's ugliness, speak to us. For most of us, however, the most constant, often chosen, and privileged hearing of the Word will be when we sit daily with the Book, the revealed Word of God. I share briefly a very simple and practical way of doing a daily *lectio*. This simple method comes from the age-old practice of the monks and nuns as expressed in their customaries.

First, *come into God's Presence and call upon the Spirit.* The old monastic usages say that, when a nun or a monk is going to do a *lectio,* he or she takes the Holy Scriptures, kneels, prays to the Holy Spirit, reads the first sentence, and then reverently kisses the sacred text. We have two elements here: coming into the presence of God dwelling in his inspired Word, and asking his Holy Spirit to help us in our *lectio.*

In the abbatial church at Spencer Abbey one always finds two lamps burning: one before the tabernacle, proclaiming the Real Presence of Christ in the Eucharist; the other over the Sacred Text enthroned in the middle of the choir, proclaiming a real presence of Christ the Word in his Scriptures. The Word abides in the Bible, ever ready to speak to us. Our Bibles should never be just put on the shelf with other books or left lying haphazardly on our desks. They should be enshrined in our homes and offices, proclaiming the Real Presence. When we come to our *lectio,* we take the book with great reverence and respond to that Presence. The monastic customarily had the monk kneel before his Lord and, after listening to his first words, kiss the text, as a sign of reverence and homage. It is good to bring even our bodies into our acknowledgment of this Presence; we are incarnate persons. Acknowledging the Lord's presence in his Word, we are ready to listen.

And we call upon the Holy Spirit to help us to hear. In his last discourse at the Supper on the night before he died, Jesus promised to send the Holy Spirit, the Paraclete, to abide with us to teach us and call to mind all he had taught us. The Holy Spirit inspired writers of the Sacred Text. This same Holy Spirit dwells in us. We ask him how to make the message, the Word of life in the text he inspired, come alive for us and truly speak to us.

Second, *listen for ten or fifteen minutes.* The length of time itself is not important, but ten or fifteen minutes can be enough for the Lord to give us a word of life. We are busy people; it is difficult for us to make time for all the things we want to do each day. But who cannot make ten minutes for something if he or she really wants to? The point here is that we listen for a period of time. The nun or monk will usually sit at the *lectio* until the next bell rings. Others do not usually have bells to summon them from one thing to another, but a time can be set. One must avoid setting a goal for oneself to read a page, a chapter, or a section. We are too programmed to speed-reading, to getting things done that, if we set ourselves to read a certain amount, we will be pushed to get it done. In our *lectio,* however, we want to be able to listen to the Word freely. If he speaks to us in the first or second sentence, we want to be free to abide there and let that Word of life resound in us, going on only when we feel we have responded to him as fully as we wish for the moment. If in our *lectio* time we hear only a sentence or two—fine! The important thing is to hear the Word, to let him speak to us.

Third, *at the end of the time, take a word and thank the Lord.* It is a wonderful thing that at any time we wish we can get God Almighty, our Lord God, to sit down and speak to us. We often have to make appointments and do a lot of waiting to get his representatives to give us some time and attention. But not so with the Lord. This moment of thanksgiving emphasizes again the real Presence. God has truly made himself available to us and spoken to us through his Word; we thank him.

And we take a word. "Word" here means a meaningful message summed up in one or a few words. In the earliest Christian times, devout women and men would go to a spiritual mother or father and ask them for "a word of life," a brief directive that would guide them in the way of Christian holiness.

> A man asked Amma Synletica, "Give me a word." The old woman said, "If you observe the following you will be saved: Be joyful at all times, pray without ceasing, and give thanks in all things."
> Abba Pambo asked Abba Anthony, "What ought I to do?" and the old man said to him, "Do not trust in your own righteousness, do not worry about the past, control your tongue and your stomach."
> Brother Bruno asked Father Basil, "Give me a word of life, Father." "Say, 'I am God's son,' and live accordingly," was the reply.

As we listen to the Lord in our daily *lectio,* we ask him for a word of life. Some days he does very clearly speak to us. Some word or phrase of the text seems virtually to shout at us. He speaks, and we hear him. Many of us have had our Taboric or Damascus moments. Such words change our lives and remain always with us, never far from our consciousness. Other times his Word is not so dramatically spoken. And on some days he seems not to speak at all. We read on and on, listening, but nothing strikes home. On such days we have to take a word and carry it with us. Often it will speak later in the day, if not for us, for another.

Guerric of Igny, a twelfth-century Cistercian monk, comments in an Easter sermon on the Gospel scene where the women who failed to find Christ at the empty tomb suddenly encounter him on the garden path. Guerric says to his brothers: You know how it is, brothers; some days we go to our *lectio* and the Lord is not there, we go to the tomb of the altar and he is not there, and then, as we are going out to work, lo, halfway down the garden path we meet him. The word we have taken may suddenly come alive for us as we are conversing with someone else, or drying the dishes, or puzzling over something altogether different.

If each day a word of the Lord can truly come alive for us and can form our mind and heart, we will come indeed to live by faith as just persons; we will have the mind of Christ. *Meditatio* has precisely this aim.

Again, I hesitate to translate *meditatio* directly. "Meditation" has come to have various meanings for us. Perhaps the most prevalent meaning is that given to it in modern English Hindu terminology, which may be a commentary on how poorly we Christians have made our own heritage present and available. We have all heard of transcendental meditation. In this Eastern sense, meditation means a certain emptiness, openness, presence to the Absolute, to the No-thingness, the Beyond, and the practices that seek to take us into such a state. In more recent Christian usage, meditation has meant searching out the facts and mysteries of revelation to understand them better, to be moved to respond to them, and to bring their influence into our lives. It has been largely a rational exercise ordered toward affective and effective response. *Meditatio* in the earlier Christian tradition had a meaning that perhaps can be seen as lying somewhere between these two modern meanings. Meditation in this tradition meant repeating the word one had received from *lectio*, whatever form it took—reading, the faith-sharing of a father, the proclamation in the assembly—repeating it perhaps on the lips, at least in the mind, until it formed the heart, until, as the Fathers sometimes expressed it, the mind descended into the heart. On a couple of occasions, Luke in his Gospel tells us that Mary pondered or weighed certain events in her heart. He is pointing toward meditation of this sort. The word is allowed simply to be there, letting its weight, its own gravity, press upon us till it gives form to the attitude of our heart. The result is *oratio*.

Oratio could be translated simply "prayer" yet we too easily think of prayer as asking God for something or conversing with him or saying prayers. These elements are indeed prayer and can be good prayer. But here, when the Fathers speak of *oratio*, they mean something different. They mean something very powerful and urgent: fiery prayer, darts of fire that shoot out from the heart into the very heart of God. As the Psalmist sings, "In my meditation fire bursts forth." It is prayer in the Holy Spirit. It is brief. It is total. When the Word finally penetrates and touches the core of our being, it calls forth this powerful response, whether it be a cry of praise, love, petition, thanksgiving, reparation, or some mixture of all of these, according to the particular word and circumstances. This response is pure prayer. For a moment it takes us beyond ourselves. It calls forth from us a response so complete that we are momentarily wholly in the response. For a moment we leave behind all consideration of ourselves, all the usual self-reflection or self-awareness; we are totally in the response. At that moment we fulfill the first and greatest commandment: we love the Lord our God with our whole mind, our whole heart, our whole soul, and all our strength.

Such moments are very special. We want them to return and to continue; in a word, we want *contemplatio*. In this tradition, the term means that the Word has so formed us and called us forth that we abide in total response. Our whole being is a "yes" to God as he has revealed himself to us. We are, as the Book of Revelation says of Christ, as Amen to the Father.

This transformation of consciousness we cannot bring about by ourselves. It is beyond us. We can prepare ourselves for it, seek it, and dispose ourselves for it. We can actively prepare for it by seeking to let go of the things that have a hold on us and keep us from being free to be a complete "yes" to God. This is the role of self-denial or mortification. Our Master spoke of taking up our cross daily, denying ourselves, and dying to self when he said that the grain of wheat must fall into the ground and die before it can bear fruit. We have to be willing to let go of self and the constant watching of self, the wanting to be right, and must turn our whole attention on God, so that we can truly and freely hear his Word through openness, letting it in and letting it reform us, through *lectio* and *meditatio*. We can dispose ourselves for transformation by making spaces for God to come in and reveal himself and, in that revealing, transform us. "Be still," he says, "and know that I am God."

God made us; he knows us through and through and respects us as no one else does. He knows the greatest thing he has given us is our freedom, because therein lies our power to love, to be like him who is Love. He respects our freedom. He will never force his way into our lives: "Behold, I stand at the door and knock. And *if* one opens, I will come in." We first open the door by *lectio;* we further open it by silent attentive presence. When the received word has informed our hearts and, through the passing experiences of fiery prayer, creates in us a desire for an abiding transformation, an abiding state of prayer in presence, we begin to want to cultivate interior quietness, silence, and space in expectant longing. The Fathers have passed down to us a method for cultivating this prayer of the heart. Centering prayer is a modern presentation of this traditional method. But no method is more than a disposition. It is a concrete way of asking, of seeking. Contemplative prayer remains a gift. We dispose ourselves in a stillness that expresses an intent loving longing. And then he comes, when he wills.

Much of our time may be spent in expectant, silent waiting. We may murmur again and again his name, our word of love and longing. But we can only wait until he comes and with his touch draws us forth beyond ourselves into the knowledge, the experiential knowledge of himself, which transforms our consciousness. When he continues to give it, this transformed state of consciousness becomes more abiding, until by his grace and mercy it quietly prevails even in the midst of our many activities. In this state of consciousness we come to see things as he sees them, value them as he values them. We seek to become full collaborators with him in bringing about by love and service the redeeming transformation of the world. I will not develop here at length the effects of this lived transformation of consciousness, but I think one can readily surmise how it will affect our relationships with others and with the rest of creation. It certainly provides the base for global community and ecological reverence.

One striking aspect of this Christian way to transformation is its simplicity. We have but to open ourselves to the revealing and all-powerful Word of God, and he will do the rest. It is simple, but not easy. For such openness implies making time and space to hear. Making time is difficult enough in our busy lives. Making space in our cluttered hearts is more difficult, for if each day we do take the next step in faithfulness to his revealing Word, in the end we will have to give up everything. But this sacrifice is only in order to have the space to find everything, in all its potential fullness and magnificence, with him and in him, no longer bound by our limitations. In this way we come to live the first great commandment—to love the Lord our God with our whole mind, heart, soul, and strength—and the second, which is like unto it, to love our neighbors and the whole creation as we love ourselves in that first great love. It is to be wholly in the way, identified with the Way, who is the Way to the Father in the Holy Spirit of Love.

CONTRIBUTORS

John E. Collins is Associate Professor of Religion, Wake Forest University.

Samuel S. Hill is Professor of Religion, University of Florida.

David J. O'Brien is Professor of History, College of the Holy Cross.

M. Basil Pennington, O.C.S.O., is Editor-in-Chief of Cistercian Publications, St. Joseph's Abbey, Spencer, Massachusetts.

Douglas V. Steere is Emeritus Professor of Philosophy, Haverford College.

Manfred H. Vogel is Professor of the History and Literature of Religions, Northwestern University.

Frank B. Wood is Associate Professor of Neuropsychology, Bowman Gray School of Medicine, Wake Forest University.

Ralph C. Wood is Professor of Religion, Wake Forest University.

John Howard Yoder is Professor of Theology, University of Notre Dame.

INDEX

Adams, John, 87
Adler, 13
Ahlstrom, Sydney, 58
Ambrose, 3, 4
Atman, 106, 126
Augustine, 12, 143

Barth, 12, 13, 95
Beecher, Henry Ward, 46
Behavioralism, 120
Bellah, Robert, 20, 22, 29-31, 61-62
Bennett, William, 97
Berger, Peter, 62, 89
Bernard of Clairvaux, 144, 157
Berrigan, Daniel, 36, 58, 59
Bill of Rights, 4, 6
Blake, William, 148
Bloom, Anthony, 147
Bohm, David, 122
Bonhoeffer, 13
Bryan, William Jennings, 10
Bushnell, Horace, 90

Callahan, David, 58
Calvin, 15
Campbell, Alexander, 10
Carroll, John, 41, 46-47, 53
Carter, Jimmy, 19
Charlemagne, 16
Cicero, 95, 98
Civil community, 2-3, 8, 14, 16, 19
Cogley, John, 58
Comblin, Joseph, 41
Commonweal, 54
Constantine, 3-4, 7, 16, 18
Constantinianism, 7-9, 99
Contemplatio, 156, 161
Court, Donald, 146
Cox, Harvey, 13, 14
Crow, T. J., 131

Declaration of Independence, 5

Disestablishment, 6, 65-67, 75, 79, 93
Dopamine, 130
Dualism, 111-13, 115
Dulles, Avery, 60
Durnbaugh, Donald, 2

"Ecclesiological type," 2
Eckhart, 140, 144
Ellis, John Tracy, 55
England, John, 42-43
Erickson, 13
Established religion, 2, 77
Establishment, 7, 8, 16, 76, 79
Exteroception, 109, 113

Fallwell, Jerry, 86, 89
Federalism, 6
Feuerbach, 12, 94
Field independence, 133-34
Fox, George, 16, 145
Franklin, Benjamin, 92-93
Free church, 15, 16
Freud, 13, 94
Fundamentalism, 90

Garrett, James Leo, 2
Garrison, William Lloyd, 10
Garvey, John, 36-37
Gibbons, James Cardinal, 47
Great Awakening, 87
Guerric of Igny, 159

Hammond, Phillip, 28-30
Hauerwas, Stanley, 98-99
Herberg, Will, 3
Hippocampus, 102-104, 107-108
Holocaust, 135
Horizontal dimension, 67-69, 74, 77-78, 80-82, 84
Horton, James E., 10
Hughes, John, 46-48

Idealism, 117-24

Idolatry, 14, 22
Input processing, 109, 114-15
Institute for Religion and Democracy, 86
Interoception, 109, 113
Ireland, John, 49-51, 53, 63

James, William, 107, 148
Jefferson, 6, 29, 88, 92, 98
John XXIII, 40, 60, 62
John Paul II, 64
Jung, 13

King, Martin Luther, Jr., 5, 10, 89
Kinsborne, Marcel, 134
Kraemer, Hendrick, 11-12

Lashley, Karl, 118, 120
Lectio, 156-61
Leo XIII, 40, 60, 62
Liberation theology, 91
Lincoln, 5, 29, 85
Lindbeck, George, 97
Littell, Franklin, 2, 10
Luther, 12
Lymbic system, 102

McCloskey, John, 43
MacDonald, George, 143
McGill, Arthur, 96
Madison, James, 88
Mailer, Norman, 35, 36, 38
Mandell, Arnold, 101-109, 112, 114, 125-26
Mann, Thomas, 148
Maritain, Jacques, 41
Marty, Martin, 1
Marx, 13, 94
Materialism (materialistic reductionism), 101-108, 117
Mead, Sidney, 9, 22, 31, 92, 93
Meditatio, 156, 160-61
Modernist condemnation of 1905, 53
Montesquieu, 61
Moral Majority, 86
Morgenthau, Hans, 19
Muggeridge, Malcolm, 60
Murray, John Courtney, 36, 55, 57

Niebuhr, H. Richard, 31
Niebuhr, Reinhold, 31, 63, 91
Nietzsche, 13, 94
Nixon, Richard, 1
Nonestablishment, 89

Norepinephrine, 130
Novak, Michael, 58, 86
Nygren, Anders, 142

Oratio, 156, 160
Orthodox Judaism, 77

Pannenberg, Wolfhart, 94
Parapsychology, 111
Parker, Alexander, 145
Pavlov's dogs, 103-105, 107
Pelagius, 12
Penn, William, 9, 15, 16
Percy, Walker, 87
Pius XI, 39
Prajapati, 124-26
Pribram-Bohm theory, 122-24
Pribram, Karl, 101, 118-24, 126

Rahner, Karl, 59-60
Rauschenbusch, Walter, 63
Reagan, Ronald, 35
Realism, 101-102, 108-18
Real Presence, 158
Ricoeur, Paul, 158
"Rights," 5
Rousseau, 87, 93

Schluter-Hermkes, Maria, 142-43
Schweitzer, Albert, 151
Serotonin, 102, 104, 108
Social Gospel, 64, 90, 91
Southern Baptist Convention, 25
Speiser, E. A., 131
Stassen, Harold, 10
Syllabus of Errors, 43-44
Sylvester, 3, 4

Tart, Charles, 101, 108-18, 125
Temple, William, 148
Theodosius, 3
"Theology of crisis," 11, 12
"Theology of word," 11
Thomas, Norman, 10
Tillich, Paul, 31, 94
Tocqueville, 43-45
Transpersonal psychology, 108-18
Troeltsch, 10
Tullig, Endel, 134

Underhill, Evelyn, 139-40

Vatican I, 51, 52
Vatican II, 57, 60

Verduin, Leonard, 7
Vertical dimension, 74-75
von Hügel, Baron, 139-40, 144
von Speyr, Adrienne, 148

Washington, 29, 88
Wave model, 118-24
Weber, Max, 28

Williams, Michael, 54
Williams, Roger, 9, 15, 16
Wilson, John F., 30
Wilson, Woodrow, 30, 33, 34
Winthrop, John, 85
Woolman, John, 141-42, 153

Zwingli, 15